KIDS LIKE ME

Praise for
Kids Like Me

"*Kids Like Me: Voices of the Immigrant Experience*
provides a valuable resource for educators, volunteers,
staff of youth organizations and parents of young people
attending schools with the 'kids' whose profiles
are so sensitively shared. Globalization's young faces
and voices come alive in *Kids Like Me*."

—**Frances Hesselbein,** former National Executive Director
of the Girl Scouts of the USA and Chairman of Leader to Leader Institute

"*Kids Like Me* is at once a delightful, timely, and very
serious contribution to intercultural relations by two
of the field's most experienced practitioners. Judee Blohm
and Terri Lapinsky offer a creative, compassionate,
informative, and ultimately very practical treatment of a
topic that is already huge in its implications and only
continues to grow in significance. Teachers, students, and
interculturalists alike will benefit from this fine book."

—**David J. Bachner, Ph.D.,** Scholar-in-Residence
and Director, Intercultural Management Institute,
School of International Service, American University

"This book is about understanding from the heart—
understanding how being 'the other' feels and helping
people who have never experienced that 'otherness'
to appreciate what being different feels like. . . . *Kids Like Me*
gives teachers meaningful and accessible ways to help them
explore complex themes with their students, to help them
recognize the pain inflicted by racism as well as recognize
opportunities for expressing kindness and valuing diversity."

—**Elizabeth Macdonald,** Director of the Writing
Enhancement Program, Thunderbird,
the Garvin School of International Management

KIDS LIKE ME

Voices of the Immigrant Experience

by Judith M. Blohm & Terri Lapinsky

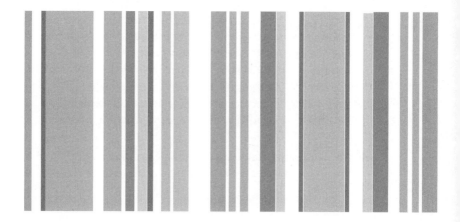

INTERCULTURAL PRESS
A Nicholas Brealey Publishing Company

BOSTON • LONDON

First published by Intercultural Press, a Nicholas Brealey Publishing
Company, in 2006.

Intercultural Press, a division of
Nicholas Brealey Publishing
100 City Hall Plaza, Suite 501
Boston, MA 02108 USA
Tel: + 617-523-3801
Fax: + 617-523-3708
www.interculturalpress.com

Nicholas Brealey Publishing
3-5 Spafield Street, Clerkenwell
London, EC1R 4QB, UK
Tel: +44-(0)-207-239-0360
Fax: +44-(0)-207-239-0370
www.nbrealey-books.com

© 2006 by Judith M. Blohm and Terri Lapinsky

Printed in the United States of America

10   09   08   07   06   1   2   3   4   5

ISBN-13: 978-1-931930-21-5
ISBN-10: 1-931930-21-X

Library of Congress Cataloging-in-Publication Data

Blohm, Judith M.
    Kids like me : voices of the immigrant experience / by Judith M. Blohm
& Terri Lapinsky.
        p. cm.
    Includes bibliographical references.
    ISBN-13: 978-1-931930-21-5
    ISBN-10: 1-931930-21-X
1. Immigrant children—United States—Juvenile literature. 2. Immigrant
children—United States—Interviews.   I. Lapinsky, Terri. II. Title.
    JV6600.B56 2006
    305.23086'9120973–dc22

                        2006003554

For my Dad and brother Steve,
Who had immense curiosity about the world
And found every new person interesting
and enlightening.
JB

For my immigrant grandparents
and my husband, Albert,
And all the others who risk the journey
and give so much.
TL

Contents

Part 1 Their Stories

Part 2 Activities and Resources

Acknowledgments

The authors wish to thank the young immigrants who were willing to share their stories and their parents for allowing them to do so. We learned from and were inspired by them every step of the way. We know that their challenges and joys, disappointments and nostalgia, are dealt with each day by the multitudes of social service workers, teachers, community members, and other dedicated individuals who assist in their transition, several of whom contributed to the making of this book.

The authors gratefully acknowledge those who helped interview the young people featured in this book or assisted us by identifying teachers, youth workers, or other committed adults who found the purpose of this book worthy and located young immigrants for us. Specifically, we thank Mark Abe, Rabbi Shmuel Afek, Julie Bartenstein, Ruth Bowman, Marshall Brewer, Susan Brock, Kathy Callahan, Basma DeVries, Anna Domenico, Steve Donohoe, Trisha Dowling, Susan Fernandez, Robbins Hopkins, Janice Johnson, Dolly Joseph, Peaches Joyal, Hank Lacy, Chuck and Sue Lapinsky, Joyce Lapinsky, Marianne LeVert, Elizabeth Macdonald, Tony Macias, Febe McLaughlin, Monica Mumford, Marc Nahmani, Barbara Pobotoy, Andrew Wilson, and Michael Wolven. We also acknowledge our many professional colleagues, students, friends, and family members who shared or pointed us to activities and resources and encouraged us.

We recognize our publisher for pursuing the desire to have a book for American young people related to the immigrant experience, and our editors for their assistance, suggestions, and their patience in making this desire come to life.

Finally, we thank everyone who takes the time to read this book... the positive things you will do with what you learn is the reason why we wrote it.

Introduction

The Kids' Stories

Kids Like Me: Voices of the Immigrant Experience is a collection of 26 stories written from interviews with young people from 23 different cultures. Most of the *Kids* range in age from 10 to 21, and a few are young adults looking back at their immigrant experience. They are like you in some ways: they live in different cities and towns across the United States, have families and friends, and may share some of your interests. They could be your classmates or neighbors. Yet, they were born outside of the U.S., and they remember and still observe some of the customs from "home"—whether their native country is Korea, Somalia, Mexico, Sierra Leone, or Moldova.

Today most Americans live in multicultural communities with residents from a range of backgrounds. Some of your neighbors may have moved to the United States to have more chances for work, whereas others might have come here for better educational opportunities. They may have fled a conflict among the peoples of their home country or a war between their home country and another. Still others come to the U.S. as a member of a blended family with one American parent or step-parent.

Read about Anne Rose, age 18, who was born in French Guyana of Haitian parents. Anne Rose's parents came to the United States years in advance of her sisters and her in the hopes of creating a life of opportunity for their family. Anne Rose advises fellow immigrants to *"Get involved in everything you can!"* Her transition to life in the U.S. was difficult but ultimately fulfilling as she followed the philosophy of *"Seek and you shall find."*

The Authors' Story

This book was written "virtually," mostly via e-mail between two long-time friends from two different backgrounds on two different continents, with the help of dozens of other adults and the immigrant kids they knew from all across the United States. You could do that with your friends too. Our goal in writing this book is to help Americans kids find out more about their immigrant classmates and the world beyond our shores, and to help young newcomers know that they are not alone or powerless as they try to make a successful transition to life in the U.S. Ultimately, we think that type of knowledge has the power to transform you—the next generation—into the kinds of adults who will make this country and the world a better place for everyone to live. You have a big job!

By listening to the "voices" of these *Kids,* you will find that you have things in common with all of them: everyone has favorite celebrations and holidays; favorite subjects in school and experiences that are hard or upsetting and ones that make them feel good. Of course there are differences: different cultural histories, different customs, different native languages, and different ways of interacting. That's part of what makes it interesting to meet new people.

The first part of the book has all of the *Kids'* stories. The stories may get you interested in exploring your own culture and learning about immigration and how people adapt to new countries. That's why there's a second part of the book. The second part has lots of activities you can do by yourself, or with your friends, family, class, or club. It mentions websites and other resources you can use to learn more about the things that interest you—and how to get more involved with them. You may find topics to use for class or club projects or research papers.

Your Story

We all have a story to tell. If you have ever moved, you probably will remember that you may not have made new friends until you had a chance to tell your story to someone, someone who was interested in where you lived before, liked some of the same things you liked, or had moved themselves.

Consider Liban from Somalia. What do you know about Somalia? Do you see stories about it on TV? Liban talks about living close to relatives and doing lots of the same activities that you do. But he also has a story of living in a country at war, where there was no school, and everyone was afraid. How would you get to know Liban without talking with him and hearing his story? He says he is very talkative…and talks with everyone. Would you be willing to talk to him?

Learning to Deal with Differences

Through these true stories, what you have read in your social studies books will come alive with the history, geography, and cultures of real *Kids* who will answer many of the questions that you have about the world. We hope this will make you want to reach out to the students around you who come from places that you have never been. When we encounter people who are different from us, we often tend to be afraid of or confused by them. In turn, we then ignore, make fun of, or avoid those people, mostly out of fear. Once we get to know people better the fear diminishes and there is a chance for understanding and friendship to begin.

When we don't understand people who are different, it is usually because we have been taught different values. As you read the stories, you will find some differences that you may have never thought about before. That is good. You will be learning more about yourself!

Jacque, who emigrated from Mexico, says that while living in the United States she learned more about being Mexican. Pang Houa, who is Hmong, mentions that when she left the U.S. for a year abroad during college, she suddenly realized how American she was!

What Is Culture?

Culture is defined in several ways. Often, we think of culture as being about music, art, religion, or history; some call this *big C* culture. In contrast, we think of *small c* culture as being about groups of people—what they believe, how they behave, and what they value. Small *c* culture is all the things we are taught by our parents, our teachers, and our religious leaders: what is right and wrong, how to behave in different situations, what is important, and so on.

What you'll find in these stories is primarily about small *c* culture. You will read about culture in the stories, and you will learn about the *value* of good relationships with other people.

- Annie describes the Moldovan braided bread that represents togetherness.
- Sanuse and Adib visited friends and relatives during the holiday of Ramadan to wish them well.
- Jeff talks about his close friendship with his five brothers.
- Noemy describes the importance of a girl's fifteenth birthday celebration.

Most of the *Kids* mention special foods or holidays with extended family as their best memory and their biggest loss when they moved to the United States. Hewan says that family meals are very important. Holiday celebrations for Tim and Pushpa primarily are times spent with extended family members and often include special food. Manuel and Jacque talk about how weekends are spent with family or visiting relatives. Roya recalls the special events of Persian New Year. Foods and holidays reflect cultural values that they strive to hold onto even as they make a new home in the U.S.

Many of the *Kids* in this book state that they have a closer relationship with extended family members than they see among their American peers, which is again a reflection of values and customs, or small *c* culture. Some, like Pang Houa, come from cultures where there are three generations of family members living in one house. Jorge states that his grandparents lived with them to help raise the kids.

Sometimes it is hard to understand culture. That's because most of it is not something you can touch or see. Can you see respect? Well, you can see how people *show* respect. Pushpa talks about how the students were taught to show respect for their teachers by standing up when a teacher comes into the classroom. How do we show respect to our teachers in the United States?

When you look in the mirror, what do you see? Try doing that and just say the answer to yourself. Is your answer *all* that you are…tall/short, blond/dark, bad haircut, nice clothes? Is your haircut considered bad outside of your neighborhood? Would you be considered tall (or short) in every country?

Keep looking in the mirror and tell yourself what you and others *can't* see…your beliefs, your ideas, your values, your good singing voice, how close you are to your family. What else? Which of the attributes that you just mentioned are things you can change? Which are things you can learn to do and share? Which are similar to others people's attributes and which are unique to you?

What Are Stereotypes?

Everyone tends to generalize, but overgeneralizations—*stereotypes*—whether positive or negative, make us feel defensive and isolated from others. We put people into categories in order to make sense of our world, to protect ourselves, to feel more secure. Yet that kind of protection often cuts us off from the many positive experiences we could have with people of different backgrounds. The *Kids* in this book tell us their dreams and help us reject stereotypes that we may have about immigrants. For example:

- Raoul is interested in politics or law.
- Anne Rose is considering social work.
- Pushpa and Hewan are hoping to go into medicine.
- Romina wants to study pharmacy.
- Na'ama wants to become a linguist.
- Inayet is interested in working in government or with nonprofit organizations.
- Naomi and Sanuse are interested in the military.
- Jennie would like to help the world by working at the United Nations or becoming a Good Will Ambassador.

As you read the stories, you will find that some of the *Kids* have stereotypes of Americans (and each other), too. Where did they get those stereotypes and why do they have them? Do you fit the American stereotype? What is an American? Where did your ancestors come from? What can you do to help kids to see Americans and each other as individuals?

Adjusting to a New Culture

One of the main themes you will discover in *Kids Like Me* is the process by which immigrants learn to live in a new culture. Through classes and activities they make new friends, who then help them improve their language and learn how to be an American kid. You'll see that

- Adib and Kim got involved in sports.
- Jacque, Eunji, and Jina continued their interests in music.
- Pushpa met her friend through a discussion about rocks.
- Ramon got involved with multicultural clubs.

In addition to finding friends through shared hobbies and sports, some of the *Kids* found themselves in a particular class with someone who became their friend. Annie became friends with Maddi, one of the first kids she met in school, and Natalia got assigned to a science project group and became close with those classmates. Some sought friends who could speak their language or were immigrants themselves, like Naomi and Romina. How did you meet your friends? Are any of them immigrants?

Adjusting to a new culture begins when a newcomer connects with someone and something meaningful—like another young person who befriends them by helping them with English or their schoolwork, someone who invites them to join a youth organization, someone with whom they can share a favorite hobby or sport, or just someone who is interested in their story. Do you think you could be that "someone" to a newcomer in your community?

As you read *Kids Like Me: Voices of the Immigrant Experience*, you will learn more about each young person's country and culture. You'll be asked to compare your life to theirs in some ways, to look for ways in which you are alike and different, and to explore new concepts through activities, discussion questions, readings, and research.

Although every effort has been made to include functioning Internet websites containing accurate and appropriate information and minimal commercial content, the authors and publishers of *Kids Like Me* cannot guarantee the continuity or accuracy of information from the websites referenced in this book.

After you read and discuss these stories and do your research on the various cultures, you might be surprised to see how much you also have learned about yourself and your own country and culture. Enjoy the book and see what you can do with what you learn!

—*Judith M. Blohm and Terri Lapinsky*

Notes to Teachers, Parents, and Other Mentors

This book is based on the premise that teachers, parents, and mentors also are learners and that children often are our teachers. Everybody has a story and there are lessons to be learned from each one. In order to help all students achieve their potential and contribute to society, whatever their background, each one must have an equal opportunity not only to learn but a chance to teach others about what matters to herself or himself and why.

Teachers and other mentors can't control the home environment and can't change a child's history. Parents don't always have a say in the way their children are treated in the classroom. Other mentors can't do much about either situation. Nonetheless, even a loving home and safe neighborhood, a good school, and competent teachers will not guarantee that all students have a level playing field from which to learn.

Most young people need to be encouraged to get engaged in their own learning and motivated to read, write, and think critically about their world. This means seeing themselves in their textbooks, having their own stories told, and having the respect and interest of their teachers, parents, and other mentors; their peers; and their communities. For children of color and/or those born in other countries, this does not always happen. Bias, prejudice, and discrimination can be overcome by positive interaction with and accurate information about those whom we perceive to be different from ourselves. This occurs person by person, family by family, classroom by classroom, and club by club.

The personal stories in this book are intended to help our youth delve more deeply into understanding the root causes that result in immigration and the range of its effects on their foreign-born peers—as well as on their own lives. Through these stories globalization takes on a face, that of the rich diversity of the global *village,* where the next generation is better prepared to contribute to a more just and peaceful world. If this book opens any doors and takes readers through some steps toward making that happen, it will have achieved its purpose.

We hope this book will help teachers to teach and students to learn more holistically about history, geography, languages, cultures, and politics. It offers a revealing set of firsthand accounts by which kids can learn through their international peers about the effects of conflicts from World War II to Vietnam to Iraq; how conquests changed world maps; how languages and names evolved; how what the United States considers to be its assistance to other countries often triggers a flood of immigration that pushes it to close its doors to some and open them wide to others. Most of the book is written to and for the youth to promote their empowerment as independent learners, group facilitators, critical thinkers, and social actors.

With the wide range of experiences described by the youth in this book, each of the stories should address at least one standard or learning objective that you are trying to help your students to achieve in subject areas such as social studies, history, geography, multicultural studies, and foreign or second language education. For example, the book clearly addresses three of the ten themes that form the framework of the social studies standards prescribed by the National Council of Social Studies (NCSS), as excerpted in the following list from *http://www.socialstudies.org/standards/stands/:*

- *Culture*—The study of culture prepares students to answer questions such as: What are the common characteristics of different cultures? How do belief systems, such as religion or political ideals, influence other parts of the culture? How does the culture change to accommodate different ideas and beliefs? What does language tell us about the culture?

- *Individual development and identity*—Students should consider such questions as: Why do people behave as they do? What influences how people learn, perceive, and grow? How do people meet their basic needs in a variety of contexts? How do individuals develop from youth to adulthood?
- *Global connections*—Students need to be able to address such international issues as human rights, economic competition and interdependence, age-old ethnic enmities, and political and military alliances. See *http://www.socialstudies.org/standards/strands/*

Lessons learned from this book can mean even more to your students or youth group members and to yourself than the achievement of such standards. So many of the young people interviewed noted the importance of an understanding teacher or mentor, of making at least one good friend, and of getting involved in at least one activity that they liked.

çlthough every effort has been made to include functioning Internet websites containing accurate and appropriate information and minimal commercial content, the authors and publishers of *Kids Like Me* cannot guarantee the continuity or accuracy of information from the websites referenced in this book.

Use the *Kids Like Me* stories, discussion questions, activities, and resources in the book as jumping off points for getting to know all the young people with whom you work. Help them to discover and share their interests and talents, to know themselves and each other even better. Especially use them to help those who need you the most: the ones from whom you hear the least, the ones who can't speak the language well, those who dress differently, who eat different foods and celebrate different holidays from the majority, the ones who have stories they're reluctant to tell. Don't hesitate to ask them questions, to visit their homes, and to invite them to yours. You'll be the richer for it, and they will never forget you.

Part 1
Their Stories

The stories you are about to read in **Kids Like Me** are the personal recollections of young people who were born in other countries—countries you may not know much about yet. You will find out many of the different reasons why they moved to the United States.

The *Kids* in this book tell you about things that are important to them. If they were very young when they left their countries, they may have just a few strong memories. Those who were older when they left share more about important historical events that affected their lives. Their stories and the discussion questions will help you see a variety of perspectives on history, culture, and adjustment to a new country.

We've asked all of the *Kids* to talk about their lives in the United States as well, and what it has been like for them to go to school here. See how that compares to what it's like for you.

Most of all, we hope you find these *Kids* worth knowing—and realize that the new kids in your schools and neighborhoods are too, each in their own way. Try to meet someone around your age who was not born in the United States and learn his or her story. Perhaps you'll make a new friend, too!

Our Round Bread Symbolizes Togetherness

Name: Annie

Age: 10

Home country: Moldova

Residence in U.S.: California

My first name is Ana. It means "to sacrifice in the name of art." My middle name is Maria, the name of Jesus' mother. It means "love for God." My mom spells it *Ana-Maria* like one name, but my dad spells it like two names, *Ana Maria.* I also have people call me *Annie,* and not *Ana.*

I live in California. I am 10 years old and I am in the fifth grade in a nice school. I am from Moldova, a country in Eastern Europe. I came here because my mother got married to an American and we came to the United States to have a better future.

In Moldova, I went to preschool in our town. I used to play with all the kids who lived around my mom's apartment and my grandma and grandpa's house. We were much closer to our neighbors and relatives there than here. We remember our relatives and those who died. We have a holiday called *The Easter of the Dead,* and we go to the cemetery to remember those who are not living. We have a special way to talk to our elders. We say

Dumneavoastra to them to show respect instead of *tu,* which is the way to say the word *you* to another kid.

For Christmas, weddings, and funerals we make a bread called *colac.* It is made out of special dough. We twist together two or three strips of dough. The bread is round and symbolizes the togetherness of our people. (That is the bread I am holding in the picture.) Generally, we meet guests with bread and salt as a symbol of our hospitality. I really like helping my mom make this homemade bread. It is so delicious. It is normal in Moldova to go to a neighbor to ask for bread or salt if you run out of it.

> We meet guests with bread and salt as a symbol of our hospitality.

My parents want me to study a lot. They say that I have to go to college to get a degree. My dad volunteers a lot at my school. We have 20 field trips, and when he gets time he drives me and my classmates on field trips. In school we do International Round Robin, which helps us to understand the cultural heritage of other people. We learned how to dance like Mexicans and how to eat with chopsticks.

My best friend is Maddi. She was one of the first persons I met in kindergarten and we have been friends for five years. After two months of being in the United States I felt much better being with the kids in my school. It was around Halloween and I was learning more and more English. I was in kindergarten and I felt like I could communicate with the other kids and play with them. Before that I once wet my pants because I didn't know how to ask to go to the bathroom. My dad had to teach me how to ask.

I might like to become a lawyer. I could do this in Moldova. I also might like to be a real estate agent, which is hard to do in Moldova. I would also like to travel, which is hard for Moldovans to do, because other countries don't like to let Moldovans into their countries, because they think Moldovans will

just stay there. Also, most Moldovans don't make very much money, which I'll need to have a good life.

Most people don't know I am from another culture, and even if they do, they don't know anything about Moldova and any stereotypes about the culture. The only stereotypes I hear are that some people think Moldova is all just farmland and that all Moldovans are farmers and work out in the fields. Moldova does have a lot of farmland and a lot of farmers, but we also have cities and factories and things like that.

Immigrants need to make more effort to get to know Americans. The kids should make friends with Americans at school. The adults should maybe talk to their neighbors. They should see what Americans do and do what they do.

Americans shouldn't judge newcomers before they get to know them. They need to be more patient with newcomers and explain things.

Questions

1. How do you show respect to your elders?

2. Name one thing your family has borrowed from a neighbor and explain why.

3. Where are your ancestors buried? Have you ever been there?

4. Ask a classmate who was born in another state or country to explain to you how to do some thing you don't already know how to do. Did you learn to do it? Why or why not?

5. Name four things about someone you are meeting for the first time that makes you think that person was born in a country other than the U.S. What are the advantages and disadvantages of making these assumptions? Why?

6. Annie's mom is from Moldova and her dad is American. Do you or does anyone you know have family members of different cultures, races or religions? What customs or traditions does each one bring to the family from their own heritage?

Research

- Research the history of Moldova. Find its capital city on a map. What do people do in Moldova besides farming? What language(s) do Moldovans speak? See *http://encarta.msn.com/encyclopedia_761566942/Moldova.html#s4*

- Learn to ask a common question in Moldovan or another foreign language and practice asking it to a friend. Learn an answer to the question! Go to *http://moldova.takingitglobal.org/home.html* (for "chatting" with Moldovan youth.)

- Annie loves her colac bread. See if you can find other countries where colac (kolach) is eaten. You can start here: *http://www.romanian-folklife.ro/Eng/RTC_09.htm*. Do you have a family tradition that includes making and eating a certain dish at a specific time of year? What is the dish and when do you eat it? Where did the recipe come from? How is it made?

- Look up this recipe for colac (kolach) on the Web: *http://www.justalotofgoodrecipes.com/k/k1023107.shtml*. With adult supervision, make it and serve it to your classmates, friends, or family.

- A young American living in Moldova says that on the Easter of the Dead, "They visit the graves of loved ones and set up huge meals of food and drink on their graves, so as to celebrate with them instead of just in honor of them." Read her other descriptions at this site *http://www.haverford.edu/newsletter/june05/moldova.htm*. Discuss your opinions about the observance with your classmates. How does it compare to your own family traditions?

Activities

Some activities related to Annie's story:

Holidays and Celebrations (in the section Cultures and Customs)

Routines and Rituals (in the section Cultures and Customs)

Home Was a Secular Country with Many Religions

Name: Raoul

Age: 18

Home country: India

Residence in U.S.: Washington

M y name is Raoul. It is a Portuguese name. We originally come from a part of India discovered by Vasco da Gama, a Portuguese explorer. It is a small island off the coast of Mumbai [Bombay] that was settled by many Spanish and Portuguese missionaries. My great-great-grandfather was a Spanish priest who came to India to convert souls but ended up marrying an Indian lady and leaving the priesthood. My name also was inspired by the actor Raul Julia, since my mother is a big movie fan.

I was born and raised in Bangalore, India until the age of five. Life in India was very simple yet very fulfilling. People are not materialistic in India and are quite happy to play hopscotch and cricket on the streets. The popular modes of transportation are bicycle and moped. I was raised in the same home as my grandparents from my mother's side. My parents divorced soon after my mother gave birth to me.

In Indian culture, respecting our elders, especially our parents and grandparents, is a top priority. Most

> Respecting our elders, especially our parents and grandparents, is a top priority.

families raise the younger ones in one household so the children never have to go to daycare. It is common to be raised by uncles, aunts, older sisters, grandparents, and sometimes even by domestic help while parents go to work. In my family we had two maids, one to do the cooking and the other to do the cleaning. My mother stayed home and looked after me until I was five.

India is a secular country with people of different religions. In most Hindu families, girl babies are not as valued as boys. Some Hindus even will kill their unborn female fetuses. Women are often oppressed as well. Since I grew up in a Catholic household, I was taught that everyone was equal and that a marriage is a partnership between a man and a woman. I feel lucky to have that Western ideology instilled into my upbringing.

We celebrate about 21 holidays in India, including all the Christian, Muslim, and Hindu festivals. Some of the big ones are Easter, Christmas, Eid-al-Fitr, Holi, and Deepavali. Exchanging food that is homemade is a typical tradition. During the Hindu holidays neighbors give us lots of Indian sweets. At Christmas time gift-giving is not a big thing. Instead, families gather together and go to church and then come home and feast on some amazing dishes, all made by family members, much like the American Thanksgiving feast here.

During *Deepavali,* which is the festival of lights, people light lamps in their yards and then set off firecrackers all night long. This is a lot of fun. During *Holi,* the festival of color, the Hindus parade in the streets, throwing colored water on people so we wear our old clothes. During *Id,* the Muslims slaughter a goat or lamb and feast on it while sharing the meat with neighbors. The Muslim dish biriyani is my favorite. All the holidays and food are celebrated with great gusto and I miss them.

We Indians are taught from a young age that we will be worth nothing without education, so education is forced on us and the pressure to perform well is very hard on students. India has a high number of teenage suicides because children are afraid of facing their parents with bad grades. Parents get very involved in their children's education and force goals on them, such as becoming a doctor (even if the kid is squeamish and hates the sight of blood) or an engineer (even if the kid is not good in math) or a lawyer (even if the kid is not a good debater or public speaker).

When I was five, my mother moved from India to Dubai, UAE (United Arab Emirates) and met her future husband there. We moved to America when I was nine years old, because my stepdad is American and he wanted to be close to his son from a previous marriage.

My mother takes us once a year to a different country so that we learn to appreciate and respect other cultures. I see other immigrants struggling with English and American kids making fun of them. I've been learning Spanish for the last five years so I can reach out to Hispanic immigrants.

Since I spoke English before coming to this country, my own transition was easier. I did have to practice the American accent though, because the educated Indians speak English with a British accent. My math and geography skills were higher than my classmates, even though I was a year younger than they, and the other students accepted me more easily because of this. I was an honors student right from the get-go.

I haven't had any challenges or disappointments yet academically except that I was put back a grade because I started school early in India (at the age of three). I was two grades ahead of the average American when I came to this country, but my mother insisted that they only put me back one grade. This is why I entered college at the age of 17.

I'm 18 years old now and I live in the state of Washington. My closest friend in the United States is Ryan. We became friends when my mother enrolled me in a soccer team. Ryan and I do not go to the same school but we are still best friends. I have other schoolmates whom I still consider to be my friends, but now that I'm in college Ryan is the only one I keep in touch with.

I am attending university with political science as my major. My dream is to become an American, which will happen in a few months. After that, I'd like to work in politics or as a constitutional lawyer. In India, the vast population of educated Indians causes great competition in most areas of advanced study. Unless you are super rich it is impossible to get into politics. I think the Indian government is corrupt and secretive, unlike the American government where almost everything is public knowledge. I like the transparency and accountability here. Also, you can actually see your tax dollars go to work in America.

I would like Americans to know that not all Indians speak like Appu on *The Simpsons,* and not all Indians are cab drivers or 7-Eleven store owners. Some of us are very highly educated in India, where we live in large homes, drive cars on mostly paved roads, and eat healthy food. We don't believe in violence and very few Indians own guns. We follow Gandhi's motto of nonviolence. But not all Indians run around wearing loincloths like Gandhi. The Christian population in India is growing.

American teachers should have more patience, tolerance, and understanding of new students. They should ask them questions rather than assume the worst or imagine some stereotype that Americans get from the media. A lot of immigrants come to this country to better their standard of living. Many also come here with advanced degrees from their own countries which are not recognized here so they have to go back to school and re-qualify. Lots of doctors and engineers have to redo their exams to work in the same field as back in their native countries. A lot of them give up higher status in their countries to start from scratch here. Showing respect for others' cultures rather than mocking them is a good thing. Being supportive by helping newcomers understand the nuances of the American culture also helps. Americans and new immigrants can learn a lot from each other.

New immigrant students should try to learn English quickly in order to integrate, and get tutors if they can. Most schools offer ESL [English as a Second Language] classes. Getting involved in some sporting activity allows you to make friends fast, especially if you're good at that sport, since sports are a big thing in this country. At the same time, new students should not be ashamed of their heritage or their homeland. They should proudly discuss their traditions and customs with their American friends so that the Americans can understand far-away cultures and be less critical.

Questions

1. Find an atlas or a globe. Do you see an island on the map that is off the coast of Mumbai, India? What is it called? Also locate Bangalore, India. Where is Dubai, UAE?

2. What does it mean to be a *secular country?* Name three countries that are secular and three that are not. What do you think are the advantages and disadvantages of living in a secular country?

3. Which holidays do you celebrate in your school? Which ones are religious holidays and which ones are national holidays? Find out what other holidays are celebrated by the students in your class. Do research to find the dates, traditions, and the food of at least one of the holidays that Raoul mentions. With your teacher, choose a custom from any holiday that is new to you and most of your classmates and celebrate it on the appropriate date.

4. What is *Western ideology?* What do you think of Raoul's description of Hindu family values and why?

5. How do you play the game of cricket? What is a moped?

6. Why might Indian parents put so much pressure on their children to perform well in school? How do you and your family feel about the importance of a good education?

7. What is a stereotype? How many can you find in this story? How can people keep from forming and passing on stereotypes?

Research

- Trace the travels of Portuguese explorer Vasco da Gama. What other countries did he "discover?" Who was living there already? See *www.fordham.edu/halsall/mod/1497degama.html.*

- Explore the ways Christmas is celebrated around the world. How similar are U.S. customs to those of other countries? What parts of the celebrations have become or are secular rather than religious?

- Find out how Raoul's favorite dish, biriyani, is made. If you can, cook it and share it with your family or friends. For biryani and other Indian recipes, look at *www.aiol.com/recipe/mutton-biryani.htm.*

Activities

Some activities related to Raoul's story:

Meaning of Names (in the section Cultures and
   Customs)

What We Learn from the Media (in the section
   Stereotypes, Tolerance, and Diversity)

Cultural Diversity Activities/Events (in the section
   Linking the Classroom to the Community)

How Do People Become U.S. Citizens? (in the section Immigration and Citizenship)

Our Town Was Made 2,550 Years Ago

Name: Eunji

Age: 13

Home country: South Korea

Residence in U.S.: Arizona

My family name means "country." Our town was first made 2,550 years ago and has the fifth largest population in Korea. My family came to the United States this year because my dad is studying in business school. So my family followed my dad.

Life in Korea is a lot stricter than here. Korean middle- and high-school rules are mostly very strict. Many schools are separated into boys-only and girls-only schools. If I was in Korea, by now I would go to a girls' middle school and wear school uniforms. Most of the rules are like this: no piercing ears or nose or anywhere, no long hair or highlights, even no colored hair pins. But in America we don't have that kind of rules.

In Korea, we use different phrases and sentences to adults and kids. We don't say their names if they are older than us. I think one important holiday is New Year. We use the lunar calendar. In New Year, all family gets together and we wear our beautiful traditional clothes. We eat a soup made out of rice cakes. It can sound weird but it's good. Some kids believe we have to eat it to get older. The best part is that we bow in a special way to adults and we get money from them. But it's just a way to celebrate that we got older because we count our age by calendar year.

Some Americans think South Korea is dangerous to live in because of North Korea, but it's not true. It's safe and peaceful. Some other people think Korea is kind of poor. But Seoul is like New York City—there are many tall buildings, and Seoul is also very crowded.

When I came to America, my best moment was my first day of seventh grade. No one noticed I was a foreign student. It felt really good and I was kind of proud of me. No one believed I came here only six months ago. The challenge I had was in language arts class. We were reading a novel that was a little hard for me. I told my teacher and she said I could read another book. I think that is how I overcame it, by asking questions.

I think the ESL program helped me very much. ESL helped me to learn English and American culture. I'm also in the National Junior Honor Society. I didn't join any activities yet but I'll join those activities soon as the school starts.

My best friend is Becca. There was a music project and Becca was in my group. That's when we started to talk and she became my friend. After that we did almost all of the group projects together. She is a really nice friend.

My parents want me to go to college in the U.S., like an Ivy League school or Stanford or U.C.L.A. Before that, I think they want me to study in a Korean foreign language high school. I want to be a fashion designer. I can go to a famous design school in America. In America there are many fashion design companies such as the Gap and Polo. So I think that's one of my dreams I can realize in the U.S.

> **Seoul is like New York City—there are many tall buildings.**

If you are new in America, I would suggest asking many questions. That way you'll learn about the person you are talking to and about American culture. Later you also will speak better English.

I would suggest that teachers and kids help new students with their homework. It's really hard to do homework when you don't speak good English or when you don't even understand what the homework is. Maybe the teachers can list all the homework and materials to bring tomorrow for the newcomer.

Questions

1. Find Seoul, Korea on the map. What is the population of Seoul?

2. Try to find a store that sells rice cakes and buy one. What do you think of the taste?

3. How do you address your parents' friends: By their first name? Mr. or Mrs.? Aunt and Uncle? Try doing it a different way. Tell your classmates how that feels and how the people reacted. How do you show respect to your elders?

4. What do you think are some advantages and disadvantages of going to an all boys or all girls school? What is an *Ivy League* school?

5. Learn to ask a question in Korean. Are there any similarities between the words in Korean and the words in English for the same question? What does that tell you about how easy or hard it might be for a Korean speaker to learn English or vice versa.

6. Take Eunji's suggestion and help a new immigrant student in your class by writing a list of

the homework and materials he or she will need
for the following day.

Research

* How old is your town? How does Eunji know that
  her town was founded 2,550 years ago? Look at
  *http://media.graniteschools.org/Curriculum/ko
  rea/history.htm.*

* Research the modern history of North and South
  Korea. Why do some Americans tell Eunji that
  they think it must be dangerous to live near
  North Korea?

* What is the *lunar calendar?* When is the Korean
  New Year? See *www.asianinfo.org/asianinfo/
  korea/cel/annual_customs.htm.*

Activities

Some activities related to Eunji's story:

Friendship (in the section Cultures and Customs)

Holidays and Celebrations (in the section Cultures
  and Customs)

What Are Stereotypes and Why Do We Use Them? (in
  the section Stereotypes, Tolerance, and Diversity)

I Don't Look Like Americans Think the Dutch Look

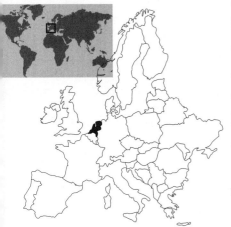

Name: Kim

Age: 14

Home country: The Netherlands

Residence in U.S.: Maryland

My name is Kim Samita. I was born in Thailand. During that time Kim was a common name in the Netherlands, and my parents really liked the name Kim too. Samita is my Thai middle name. I got it because my parents wanted me to have a Thai middle name. In Thailand most people can choose a Thai middle name that corresponds to the day of birth. Of course you can choose between different names, but my parents thought that Samita would suit me. Samita means "joyful, happiness, and smile."

I have Dutch nationality, which means that I come from the Netherlands. Although I wasn't born in Holland, and I have lived more outside of the Netherlands, I still consider myself Dutch. This is because my parents and my whole family is Dutch. I have a Dutch passport, I speak the Dutch language, I follow Dutch traditions, and I have Dutch habits.

I have lived in different places around the world, and have seen a lot of different aspects of the world that I had never known before. Moving is fun, although you always have pros and cons. The good thing about moving is that you get to learn more about the world, and you might even learn a new language. Of course the bad thing is leaving your family and friends behind.

I have lived in Thailand, Venezuela, and the Netherlands, and this is my second year living in the U.S. We moved here because my dad got another opportunity to go abroad for a job. I live in Maryland. I attend a really nice and a good school. I like it a lot.

I have lived in Holland for a total of three years. My favorite holidays in Holland are Sinterklaas, Christmas, and New Year's Eve. *Sinterklaas* is a holiday that we celebrate on the 5th of December, and children get lots of presents. Christmas is a great time for family to get together to eat dinner and talk. In Holland we have two Christmas days. New Year's Eve is a lot of fun in Holland with a lot of great fireworks.

The different taboos I have seen in Venezuela, Thailand, and the Netherlands are comparable to the U.S.; however, one country is more liberal or more tolerant than the other. The following are some examples:

* In the Netherlands the possession of small quantities of soft drugs such as marijuana and its use is tolerated. In the Netherlands they look at this issue more from a health point of view. They compare soft drugs to other health risks, like those of alcohol and tobacco use, while in the U.S. law enforcement plays a dominant role to fight against it.

* In the U.S. you are allowed to drive when you are 16, which is against the law in Holland, Thailand, and Venezuela. It is strictly forbidden to drive a car under the age of 18 in these countries, since they consider the risks of accidents very high when minors drive cars.

My parents are very supportive towards my education. It's their and my first priority. They expect me to get good school results, so they have high expectations. They know that I would like to become a doctor so they support me in every way to reach my goal. We regularly go to the library to check out books to help me with projects, research papers, etc. My mother is very involved in school activities and knows her way around the school. My parents also promote me to get involved in sports and music, which I like very much.

When I was living in Venezuela, I got an idea of what I wanted to be in the future. I was about 10 years old. It all started when I had plastic surgery to remove five small moles. When I was getting the surgery I was awake and saw what the surgeon was doing. He asked me what I wanted to be. I have always liked to help people, so I said that I would probably want to become a doctor. So he started telling me how much fun being a doctor is, although it's a lot of work and studying, but when you are totally done you will be happy that you are a doctor. So he got me interested.

While he was removing the mole on my hand, he would show me and tell me all about it. Afterwards he asked me if I wanted to stitch it up. So I said yes, and he showed me how to do it. It was really interesting, and since that time in the operating room I have wanted to become a doctor. I still have no idea what kind of doctor, maybe a pediatrician. Up to now I have realized my dreams and I hope that my wish to become a doctor comes true.

I'm very active in extracurricular activities, both at school and outside. I play clarinet, piano, saxophone, and flute. Because of these abilities I also play in the school band. I also do track and field as an after-school activity, and I have private tennis lessons and acting classes. I like to play sports and to be active. I want to be in shape and like to feel fit, so by doing sports I'm always in a good mood. I also enjoy going to the movies and socializing with my friends.

I have a lot of best friends living around the globe. In the U.S I have two best friends to add to my circle of friends. One of my best friends came to the U.S the same time I came here, so we were both new to the school. She is half Brazilian and half Argentinean, but she has lived in Texas for a while. We had almost all of our classes together, so we got to know each other very well in the first year.

Then during a science project we had to work in groups of three, so we needed another person in our group. So a girl came up to us and asked us if we needed a third person. She is my other best friend. She was born in Miami, but has lived here for almost her entire life. Both her parents come from South America. Her mom is Cuban and her dad is Venezuelan. So this also meant that she speaks Spanish. She has been at my school for almost 11 years now and still likes it.

While working on the science project we all three clicked, and started to get to know each other better. Since then we became like the Three Musketeers.

I'm at an international school, which means that a lot of other students were in the same position as I was. Therefore the teachers understand how difficult it sometimes can be, so they know how to handle it. At the beginning of the school year, the school organizes a lot of welcome meetings for newcomers, so that they can meet up with other students to make new friends. That is exactly what I did. My friends gave me a tour around the campus and made me meet my new teachers and other people.

I have learned that the average American does not know much about other cultures. I've heard that

> Everybody is the same, no matter what color, religion, background, or education.

less than 10 percent of U.S. citizens have a passport. Most Americans think that Dutch people have blond hair, blue eyes, and a light skin color. This is not always true. I'm the total opposite: I have brown hair and eyes and I'm very tan (which is my natural skin color). Personally I do not like people who stereotype or stigmatize. Everybody is the same, no matter what color, religion, background, or education, as long as they respect law and order and other people.

When coming to a new country you will always have to get used to it. But the most important thing is to have a good start. Be happy and see the positive sides of the country. Have an American friend who knows the way and can give you good advice or is able to help you out with new things.

Meeting your neighbors will be one of the first steps. Another step would be to get settled in your home, get to know the neighborhood, know the infrastructure, etc. Try to find a sports club and other community organizations to meet new people.

It also depends on where you go in the U.S. Some places are really green, such as the area where I live. You should enjoy the beautiful nature and be outside for all kinds of sports. Have a barbeque once in a while, relax, and enjoy the beautiful weather (in summer that is).

Americans are very open and say whatever they want to say, so if you are at school, don't be too shy, give your opinion, and present yourself by doing things you like.

I would suggest that American teachers, parents, and students should know that America is not the only reference. They should respect other cultures, better understand these cultures, and adapt good customs from other countries, like eating habits and other points of view. The U.S. is known for unilateral decisions, so multilateral cooperation for global issues could be a challenge for many Americans. I dare to say this, because I have lived in other countries and grew up in different cultures.

* * * * *

Questions

1. What languages are spoken in the Netherlands? Why?

2. Have you ever moved? If so, do you share Kim's enthusiasm for new experiences?

3. How did Kim's doctor influence her decision about her future? Who has influenced what you would like to become and why?

4. Do you think that Americans are *open?* Do you say whatever you want to say? Why or why not?

5. What is a *unilateral decision?* Do you agree with Kim's idea of the U.S. role in global issues? Why or why not? Where do you think Kim got that impression?

6. Do you think that "everyone is the same…as long as they respect law and order and other people?" Why or why not?

7. Have a debate in your class about the pros and cons of legalized driving by the age of 16.

Research

* Find out more about the Netherlands, its history, and the Dutch-India/Asia connection at *www.iamsterdam.com*

* Is Kim correct about how many Americans have passports? That most know little about the rest of the world? If it is true, why might it be so?

Activities

Some activities related Kim's story:

Living in a Global World (in the section Linking the Classroom to the Community)

What Are Stereotypes and Why Do We Use Them? (in the section Stereotypes, Tolerance, and Diversity)

Together We Have a Fuller Picture (in the section Stereotypes, Tolerance, and Diversity)

Brazil Is Not Only about Soccer

Name: Natalia

Age: 14

Home country: Brazil

Residence in U.S.: Virginia

My name comes from Natal, which means "Christmas" in Portuguese. Even though I am Christian, my mom named me Natalia because it was a typical name from Brazil and she thought it was a nice name.

I'm originally from Sao Paulo, Brazil. My family and I moved to the U.S. because my dad got transferred. My dad, who was also born in Brazil, is an energy consultant. My mom used to work as a teacher but she quit because she wanted to take care of me. All of our family already knew how to speak English before moving to the States, so that made it easier to interact with people. We are probably going to stay in the U.S. and become citizens because we have no plans for going back to Brazil.

When I was growing up in Brazil, I really enjoyed the *Festa Junina.* It is a festival where people dress as laborers from the plantations and countryside. There you can dance to typical folk music, eat typical food, and play many different games. This was a place to get together with your friends and family. My favorite holidays were Christmas and New Year because that was when I would meet my family that lived in Argentina and in another city in Brazil.

My favorite food in Brazil was *pao de queijo,* which is a cheese bread formed in balls. Another very popular food from there that I loved was *brigadeiro.* This is a type of candy made of chocolate paste covered with little chocolate bits.

The relationships between the members of the family are very strong in Brazil. For example, we would always have breakfast and dinner at the same time, but here in the U.S., lots of families don't get together to eat.

Now we live in the state of Virginia. I attend high school there and take English, Spanish, and Japanese. I am fluent in English, Spanish, and Portuguese. I'm taking Japanese because I had already learned a bit of it in Brazil from our babysitter and my mom didn't want me to lose what I had learned. My parents want me to get a balanced education. This is why they have put me in private schools in Brazil and in the U.S all of my life. They value good education and spend a lot of money on it.

Kim and Carolina are my best friends. We became friends because we were put together as partners in a science project at the beginning of the year. My favorite subject in school is biology, so I would like to work with either plants or animals. I think that either in Brazil or in the U.S. I could realize that goal.

> Brazil is not only about soccer, Carnaval, the Amazon, and beaches.

There are a lot of foreign kids at my school. There are more diverse cultures and languages there, so it was easier to fit in. When I lived in Texas, there were not many different cultures there, making it a bit harder to be accepted by most kids. I felt most accepted when the kids would talk to me and not pass by me as if I were "just another new kid."

I love sports. I play soccer, basketball, and do track and field during the school year. I also love

horseback riding. Since I was a little girl I have always wanted to be a farmer and own many horses. I still would like that, but I know it won't happen because I would need to get a good job to own a farm. Since I like animals, I might want to be a veterinarian when I grow up. I have had many different kinds of pets, including dogs, chickens, hamsters, rabbits, fish, and others when I lived in Brazil. Now that I live in the U.S., I don't have any pets. The closest thing I have to a pet is my neighbor's dog, which I walk every day.

Even though it is much safer and easier to live in the U.S., I want to go back to Brazil and live there some day.

I think Americans should know that Brazil is not only about soccer, Carnaval [Mardi Gras], the Amazon, and beaches. There are many other things about Brazil that they should know. For example, in Brazil there is a mixture of many races. In the south of Brazil, there is a region inhabited by German descendents and Italians. They have their own customs and typical European towns. Brazil is also the place that has the largest Japanese population outside of Japan.

Americans should learn more about the cultures of foreign students, be in contact with them, and ask them about their life in other countries. Foreign students should learn to speak English to be able to communicate. They should join clubs and interact with other people.

Questions

1. What languages do you speak besides English? How did you learn another language? Why?

2. What festival do you know of or celebrate where everyone wears costumes representing another group of people or time in history? If

you have visited a "living museum," where there are costumed interpreters who help you understand a period of history, what did you learn by participating in the activities and eating the foods?

3. What were your stereotypes of Brazil? Where did they come from? What new information did you get from Natalia that changes your idea of what Brazil is like?

4. Natalia liked holidays where she could see family members from other cities and even another country. Where is Argentina? Why do you think Natalia might have family members there? Do you have family members in other cities? States? Countries? If so, why do you live so far apart?

5. Natalia has a couple of ideas how her love of animals could lead to a career. What kind of work do you think you want to do? Why?

6. Since Natalia says that it is much safer and easier to live in the U.S., why do you think she wants to go back to Brazil and live there some day?

7. Is there somewhere else in your state, country, or the world that you would like to visit or live? Why or why not?

Research

• Why does Brazil have the largest Japanese community outside of Japan? Research the history of the Japanese community in Natalia's hometown of Sao Paulo, Brazil, or the history of the German or Italian communities there.

• *Brigadeiros* are easy to make. Try the recipe at this Brazilian website (see if you can find someone to help you translate it!): *www.receitase menus.net/brigadeiros.html.*

Activities

Some activities related to Natalia's story:

Your Family's Immigration/Migration History (in the section Immigration and Citizenship)

Pets (in the section Cultures and Customs)

Who Is Coming to the U.S. Now? (in the section Immigration and Citizenship)

How Do People Become U.S. Citizens? (in the section Immigration and Citizenship)

I Didn't Know a Word of English When I Came Here

Name: Manuel

Age: 16

Home country: Peru

Residence in U.S.: Arizona

I am Manuel. My name comes from Spain and it reflects my Hispanic heritage. I am originally from Peru. I moved to the U.S. in order to have a better education and have more possibilities to succeed in life. Unfortunately, my family couldn't come with me. My parents are really busy working in Peru and taking care of my eight-year-old brother. I live with my aunt in Arizona. My aunt works for American Express, and she has her Bachelor's degree. My aunt is an American citizen. I have two cousins my same age here in the U.S.

In Peru I went to school, but most of the time I played soccer with my friends and ate *ceviche* all the time. My favorite food is ceviche. It's the most popular food in Peru. Ceviche is based on seafood but has mostly fish in it. Since ceviche is seafood we don't eat it at night. I don't know why.

Christmas is the holiday when I miss Peru the most. On Christmas Eve the whole family gets together at my grandmother's house early in the evening, but we wait until midnight (Christmas) to say "Merry Christmas" and give the gifts.

Carnavales was a tradition I used to celebrate with my friends every Sunday in February when I was growing up in Peru. In Carnavales people often go to the beach and that is what my family and I did too. Since February is the hottest month in Peru, we throw water on everyone! That tradition doesn't have any meaning, but it is an excuse to throw water on whomever you want.

On July 28 and 29 (Peru's Independence Day celebration) every house or building should have a Peruvian flag, otherwise they'll have to pay a fine.

The norms, values, and taboos I learned in Peru are still the same for me even though I live in a foreign country. I think there is more violence in Peru than in the U.S., especially at sporting events. In Peru, I think like in any Hispanic country, family is the main value. Families always get together on the weekends or at any holiday. The people in the communities in Peru are closer to each other than in the neighborhoods in the U.S. Because of the poverty in Peru, people are more helpful to each other. Poor people don't have enough money to spend on their daily needs, so people try to find a way to help each other, like selling food at very cheap prices.

My family and I believe that education is the primary thing I should be focusing on at this moment. Depending on how I do right now at school is going to determine how my life will be in the future. I am in the 11th grade now. I didn't know a word of English when I came three years ago, but I learned by going to school and interacting with American kids.

Armando is my best friend. He is from Mexico. I met him in eighth grade. We were both learning English and lived close to each other. We became friends because we were in the same classes and liked the same sport (soccer). I am involved in my school's soccer team with friends from other countries and different cultures. I have a lot of friends who were born in the U.S., too.

My classmates tried to become friends with me when they found out that I was from Peru. They wanted to know how it feels to have a friend who has different ideas and beliefs.

My dreams are to finish preparing for my business career and to become a professional soccer player. I want a business career as a backup, because if I am a soccer player, I want to invest and take care of my own money. I want to be a soccer player because I am kind of good at it and I want to represent Peru at a World Cup. Maybe I could become a soccer player in Peru, but it is really hard to find a job there. I want to stay in the U.S., but I also want to go back to Peru to visit.

I want people to know that Peru is a completely different country and has a different culture compared to Mexico. Peru is different in the way we speak, our food, and how we think. I want people to know that I think my culture is beautiful as any other, but different at the same time. I haven't been in Mexico, but I know that other people have wrong stereotypes about Mexicans.

I would suggest to those born in America not to stereotype or make assumptions about other people. I haven't encountered any stereotypes because people in the U.S. don't seem to know a lot about the Peruvian culture. I think schools should teach more about countries and cultures, though, so students' thinking is accurate instead of through prejudice.

For kids who move to America from other countries I have one piece of advice: Don't be lazy!

> I think my culture is beautiful as any other, but different at the same time.

Questions

1. What do you know about Peru? What do you think are the reasons that you know so much or so little about that country?

2. Why do you think Manuel is so concerned about stereotypes if Americans don't have any stereotypes about Peru?

3. Describe how you would feel if you had to leave your family and your country in order to realize your dreams. How did Manuel's experience compare to Hewan's (see the next story).

4. Find a recording of some traditional Peruvian flute music. Close your eyes and listen to it and try to imagine what Peru looks like. In pairs, describe your vision to your classmate.

5. Do you have relatives living near you? If so, do you get together with them every weekend? If not, what do you do on weekends?

6. Do you play soccer or watch soccer games on TV? Where in the world is soccer a popular sport? What is the World Cup?

7. What do you think of Manuel's plans for the future? What are the advantages and disadvantages of a career in profesional sports?

Research

• Do some research on the life story of Peruvian President Alejandro Toledo. In small groups, act out his story. If you were a young Peruvian, how do you think you would feel about that story?

• Do some research and write a page about the Peruvian city of Cuzco. Make a drawing of the city.

- In case you want to try it, a recipe for Peruvian ceviche is at *http://whatscookingamerica.net/Ceviche.htm*

Activities

Some activities related to Manuel's story:

Your Family's Immigration/Migration Story (in the section Immigration and Citizenship)

Holidays and Celebrations (in the section Cultures and Customs)

What Are Stereotypes and Why Do We Use Them? (in the section Stereotypes, Tolerance, and Diversity)

I Will Probably Get to Marry Whom I Choose

Name: Hewan

Age: 16

Home Country: Ethiopia

Residence in U.S.: Washington

My name is Hewan, which is the equivalent of "Eve" or "the first woman on earth." It is a very common name used by Orthodox Christians in Ethiopia. I am from Addis Ababa, the capital of Ethiopia. My mother, older brother, and I came to the U.S. three years ago when I was 13. We moved here to further my education goals with the help and sponsorship of my uncle. I live in the state of Washington and I am a sophomore in high school.

My life in Addis Ababa was that of a normal middle-class person, although we had domestic help, so I wasn't used to doing a lot around the house until I came here. I went to a private Catholic school. The typical class size would be about 80 to 90 students per class, unlike here where the classroom size is about 20 to 25. After eighth grade in Ethiopia, it is mandatory to learn English.

Education has always been given top priority in my family. That is why I am here in the U.S.—to get a higher education of world class standards. Getting into medical school is my goal and my family is very supportive of this. My dream is to become a heart surgeon. My mother moved to the U.S. leaving behind my father and two other sisters to allow me to follow my dream. If I were back home, I would not have that opportunity because the competition is so stiff and chances of my getting into medical school in Ethiopia would be so slim. In Ethiopia only 10 percent of those who apply for medical school pass the entrance exam.

Next month my father and sisters will be joining us in the U.S. Our family will finally be reunited after three years of separation.

Compared to Ethiopian families, American families do not seem that close-knit. We share our food from one big plate. The entire family sits around the table and eats out of one dish. Food is very important to Ethiopians, and all our social events are centered around good food. Americans tell me that they think we eat all sorts of wild animals from the jungle. This is not true. We eat normal food, like lamb, chicken, and beef, cooked in our traditional Ethiopian style. Our food can be spicy but it is also very tasty because we use lots of aromatic spices. Easter is the biggest celebration in Ethiopia. I miss that holiday very much.

> We are raised with strict codes of discipline, and as long as we live under our parents' roof, we have to obey them.

In Ethiopia, parental permission is needed for everything. Children are far more respectful of their elders and figures of authority in Ethiopia. We are raised with strict codes of discipline, and as long as we live under our parents' roof, we have to obey them. Sex is taboo and not allowed before marriage at all. Marriage is never discussed with school-going children. Since I am a Christian, I will probably get to marry whom I choose. In America, it seems like there is too much freedom, which is abused.

Amharic is the main language spoken in Ethiopia, and I teach this language to American-born Ethiopians. In addition, through my church, I also help Ethiopian kids who are born and living here in

the U.S. to understand and appreciate our customs and traditions back home. There are a lot of Ethiopians who attend my church.

In order to understand us and our culture, we would prefer that Americans ask us questions rather than criticize or assume the worst. For example, we wear our clothes more than one or two times before wshing them if they are not dirty. Just because our clothes are re-worn two or three days in a row does not make us unhygienic. We are conservative about water and detergent and clean things only after they are dirty.

Americans should also try and taste our food and be open to experiencing parts of our culture. You should not make fun of our accents, because when we first come to this country it is hard enough trying to learn the language and customs of a foreign country without being ridiculed.

New immigrants/residents to the U.S. should quickly make friends with understanding and kind Americans in order to learn the language and culture. With their help, like I got from my friend Keisha, it is easier to settle into a new country and adapt to the different customs and ideas. Keisha is my best friend in the U.S. She looked out for me when I first entered seventh grade in middle school here in the U.S. My English was nonexistent and she helped me to understand the teacher when I could not figure out what was being asked of me.

Keisha became my language teacher and interpreter until I got acquainted with the language and we have remained good friends ever since. By eighth grade I started getting awards for academic achievement and English proficiency, as my English had improved beyond normal standards. I read 350 English books in seventh grade to better my language skills.

At the same time, it is also wise to make friends with kids who have just immigrated from other countries so that we can support each other through the transition of adapting to American life.

Students should talk to us without making assumptions about us and our culture, and the same goes for teachers. Teachers have the resources to research our country and culture via the Internet before we get into their classrooms. They should be more open to the world outside of America. Parents of our American friends should know that we are not here to cause trouble but to do better and work hard to achieve the American dream just like any other American immigrant. By the same token, Ethiopian parents should be more open to American ideas too so that we can adjust to all the changes and feel comfortable.

Questions

1. What is *Orthodox Christianity?* Where is it practiced?

2. If you had a dream to pursue in another country, how would you feel if you had to leave behind one of your parents or a sister or brother in order to do that?

3. Try to cook and serve a traditional Ethiopian meal, sitting in small groups. Try to use your bread as a "utensil" to pick up your food the way it is done traditionally in Ethiopia. How do you feel about having everyone eating off of one plate?

4. We all want to protect our environment from chemical detergents and not waste water. Why then would people make fun of students such as Hewan who do not change and wash their clothes until they are dirty?

5. What does Hewan mean when she says "I will probably get to marry whom I choose?" What do you think about that?

6. What is "too much freedom" for you?

7. Learn to say hello, how are you, and thank you in Amharic. How does it feel when you have to say those words in front of other Americans? In front of Ethiopians?

8. Have you ever tried to help a new student who didn't speak English, similar to the way in which Keisha helped Hewan? How did the student react? How did you feel?

9. What stereotypes does Hewan have about Americans? Where did she get those stereotypes? Write a letter to Hewan to explain how you feel about what she has said.

Research

- Use the following websites to do some research on Ethiopia:

  www.ethiopiantreasures.toucansurf.com
  www.selamta.net/culture.htm

- Many students come from other countries to attend American colleges and universities. Try to find out how many foreign students currently attend U.S. colleges and universities and some reasons why they come. How many are in U.S. medical schools?

Activities

Some activities related to Hewan's story:

What Are Stereotypes And Why Do We Use Them? (in the section Stereotypes, Tolerance, and Diversity)

Who is Coming to the U.S. Now? (in the section Immigration and Citizenship)

Buddies and Sponsors (in the section Linking the Classroom to the Community)

We Cleaned Our Own Classrooms and Grounds

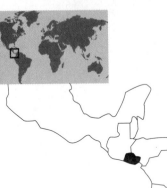

Name: Jorge

Age: 18

Home country: El Salvador

Residence in U.S.: Maryland

> We lived in close communities where everyone knew each other.

My name is Jorge and I'm from El Salvador. My last name comes from my grandmother's family.

I came to the U.S. when I was 15. My mother had already been living in the U.S. and she wanted me to come. Now my younger sister lives here, and I also have other family, like cousins, living here. We are in the U.S. because there are better opportunities for work and a better education than at home.

I love El Salvador, though. It's the best! It was great growing up there. I lived about one-and-a-half hours from the capital city. We lived in close communities where everyone knew each other, there wasn't much traffic, and there was a lot of freedom for kids to move around safely and freely. People didn't use credit cards at stores; there were small stores near our houses, and we would pay cash or just get what we needed and pay the next time.

We grew lots of our own food in a big garden that was fairly far from the house. I would only go there on weekends or on school holidays to help. The garden was fenced to keep animals out; if they got in, they'd eat everything! We grew corn, different kinds and sizes of beans, and grain. We got mangoes, bananas, plantains (big bananas that are cooked), avocados, and coconuts from our own trees or trees growing wild. My grandmother made cheese from cow's milk, and we would sell the water left over from making the cheese to people who raised pigs; pigs drank that water for food. We drank goat's milk, too, but we didn't make cheese from it.

We had lots of good sweets. They were made from different things like sweet potatoes and coconut, brown sugar, whipped eggs and sugar (sort of like the spun sugar [cotton candy] you have here), and sugar cane. Chewing on sugar cane was great; it was really juicy, sweet, and refreshing!

I was first a Catholic, and then Mormons came to El Salvador and my grandmother became a Mormon. I liked to go to the church when I was little because you got to dress up formally. Then I decided I didn't want to do it any more. Here I sometimes go to a Protestant church. It is different because there are classes for different age groups, and you can learn to play the guitar and sing with the choir; sometimes there are field trips for fun. Baptism is very different because you go under the water, and you choose when you want to join the church—you can wait until you are older.

One of our holidays in El Salvador was Holy Week, which is around the time of Spring Break here. We were supposed to stay home and be careful, because it was bad luck to hurt yourself during that week. At Halloween we would buy masks and scare people so they would give us candy. We celebrated Christmas on two days: December 25th was a time for a big family dinner and on December 31st we got presents. Fireworks were easy to buy and there were fireworks on most holidays. There was a day for cleaning the graveyard and leaving flowers, but I didn't like going to the graveyard. Some friends and I had a creepy experience there once—something threw partially eaten mangoes at us, and we could not find out where they came from!

Some of our values include respecting our elders, always offering a visitor food, and if you are offered food, to always eat it. I think we have Catholic values, and we were always to try and look at things from the other's point of view. We always want a better life for the next generation and a better education.

School in El Salvador was pretty different than it is here. I went to a public school that had students from first to ninth grades. All of our classrooms and playing fields were enclosed within a wall, and once you went in to school, you stayed there until the end of the school day. (Unless you climbed the wall to run away for a day!) The only security person was at the gate. Students stayed in the same classroom all day. For grades one through six, one teacher taught everything. Starting with seventh grade, we had different teachers for each of our seven subjects, and the teachers moved from room to room. We had about 15 minutes between each class. We would go out and eat snacks—our own types of "junk food."

The school day was from 7:00 A.M. to 1:00 P.M. That was good because it was really hot there. After school, children from different classes would do chores at the school. We cleaned our own classrooms and grounds, and there was a lot of dust (or mud if it was rainy) because outside of the classrooms it was not paved. In the afternoons, you also could ask for help from teachers if you needed it. If you were punished for something, you were assigned more chores—like coming to school before school started to sweep out the classrooms.

We wore uniforms at school: blue pants and white shirts. Our classes usually had 45 students in them at the beginning of the year, but some kids would stop coming and we'd end up with about 35.

We would eat before going to school. Our grand-parents lived with us to help raise the kids. They would usually fix breakfast.

If we didn't have chores after school, I would hang out with my friends, at one of their houses, play soccer, lift weights, or whatever we wanted to do. I loved to go hunting with a slingshot. There were lots of open areas we could explore and we often walked several miles. We would hunt for rab-bits, pigeons, other birds, iguanas, or termite hills. Termite grubs were great, as were iguana eggs. We would take the grubs home and toast them on the griddle where we cooked tortillas or put them in scrambled eggs. Iguana eggs were really rich, sort of like the yokes of other eggs.

I often didn't get home until 7:00 P.M. and my mother would say she had been worried, but she knew I was safe. If I came home after 7:00, though, I would get grounded or not get money for snacks. We didn't get an allowance. If we wanted money for something we would ask. If they had money, our parents would usually give us what we needed.

My family and I live in Maryland. I had a problem with English when I got here but I didn't give up and in four months I was speaking it! I really wanted to learn the language when I got to the U.S., because when my mother talked to people in English, I couldn't understand. She didn't want to tell me what she said. So I started watching car-toons on TV. I found I could learn English that way! If I hadn't come to the U.S., I would not have learned English or about the culture and history of the U.S.

I stopped watching TV in Spanish because I could always learn new words by watching programs in English. Sometimes now I know a word in English but don't know the same word in Spanish. That is really strange. I don't want to forget Spanish, though, so we speak Spanish at home.

I am a senior in high school now. My favorite class is an elective course in ceramics. It's really fun. I have made several things, including a little vase that Mom really likes. The teachers in the U.S. are awesome because they are nice and help you understand.

I belong to an after school club called LUCHA, which means "fight" in Spanish. The letters stand for words, but I can't remember them except for *L* which stands for *Latin*. It is a club primarily for Spanish-speaking kids from various countries, but others can join too. It is mostly run by kids, and we organize activities, raise money for field trips, eat foods from different countries, and do other things. We share news with each other, and those who need help get tutoring from other kids in the group.

I love fixing things and I'm good at it. I like motors and other mechanical things. My dream is have two auto mechanic places, one here and one in El Salvador. I'll stay here and hire people to work in my shop in El Salvador. You can earn good money being a mechanic.

I would like Americans to know that just because we come from a different country doesn't mean that Americans should think that they are better than we are.

I think everyone should just be themselves. Teachers and others should not make newcomers feel like they are alone. Try to be friends with them and hang out and stuff. Don't embarrass them because all that does is make them shut down.

Questions

1. Why do you think it is important to Jorge that he not forget how to speak Spanish? What languages do you speak other than English? How do you keep from forgetting the other language(s)?

2. Jorge lived in the countryside in El Salvador. How does his description of rural living compare to rural life in the U.S.? Name some similarities and differences in the chores, the family relationships, the animals, and the food.

3. What are iguanas and termite grubs? What things do you eat that most of your friends will not eat? Try to eat something different for the first time. If you like it, get your family and friends to try it!

4. Look at paragraph three where Jorge says why he loved living in El Salvador. How is his description the same or different from the way you would describe life in your home town? Why do you think that is?

5. Jorge has identified skills he is good at that could lead to his future work. Do you know what you are good at doing? How could you use those skills in jobs in the future?

6. Jorge tells us that when young newcomers get embarrassed at school they might "shut down." What do you do when you are embarrassed? How do you get over it?

7. Jorge was born in the 1980s. What was happening in El Salvador at that time? How might these events have influenced the immigration of Salvadorans to the U.S.?

Research

- Learn about the recent natural disasters that happened in El Salvador, the first one in 1998 and the second one in 2001, the year that Jorge moved to the U.S. See *http://news.bbc.co.uk/1/hi/world/americas/country_profiles/1220684.stm.*

- Jorge says that in El Salvador several students would leave school during the year. Why do you think that happened? Do students ever drop out at your school? Why or why not? (See *http://www.hrw.org/children/labor.htm* and *http://www.stopchildlabor.org/index.html*)

- Jorge has worshipped in the Catholic, Mormon, and Protestant traditions. All of these are Christian religions, but what are some of the differences in the beliefs and customs of each one? You can start learning here: *www.lightplanet.com/mormons/.*

- All countries have immigrants who came from other lands. Find out how and why El Salvador has a president of Palestinian descent. Go to *www.bethlehemassoc.org/sub_pages/ElSalvador_DailyStarArticle.htm.*

Activities

Some activities related to Jorge's story:

Holidays and Celebrations (in the section Cultures and Customs)

Family Rules (in the section Cultures and Customs)

Who Is Coming to the U.S. Now? (in the section Immigration and Citizenship)

If We Do Well in School, It's a Reward for Ourselves

Name: Na'ama

Age: 16

Home country: Israel

Residence in U.S.: Arizona

My name is Na'ama and I am from Israel. Na'ama is the Hebrew name of the wife of Noah (the guy with the ark) and my parents really liked that name. I was born two weeks after the *parasha*—the "chapter" in the Bible—where Na'ama is mentioned. This name reflects my heritage because it's biblical and I am a Jewish religious girl (although not only religious Israelis name their daughters Na'ama).

My grandparents were born in Yemen. I don't know what year they immigrated to Israel, but they were little kids, so they speak Hebrew and they're like original Israelis. Both of my parents were born in Israel and so was I. My parents moved to the U.S. when I was 14 because they were sent here by a Jewish agency that sends Israelis to many countries in the world to teach Hebrew and Judaic studies. We live in Arizona, and I'm a junior in high school now.

Many things were very special to me in Israel: Yemenite food like *malawach* (hard to pronounce but yummy) that my grandmother and my mom make so well, and all the Jewish holidays are very important to me and I always observe them even in the U.S.

The Israeli culture is very open and straightforward. That is one of the many things I like about it. This contrasts with American values in that Americans can be (I'm sorry I'm saying this, not to offend anyone) very fake. They usually are not as open as the Israelis. Israelis are not rude. They're just honest and do not mean to hurt. Americans, on the other hand, can hurt you but with a smile on their face, but that is equally offending/hurting.

Like they say, Israelis are like *sabra* (the fruit of the cactus): We seem rude and unpleasant when you look on the outside, but once you open and look deeper we are very warm, helping, and caring people. Israelis are very close with each other and always help each other.

I've always felt accepted because of my attitude. I don't let anyone bring me down even if they make fun of my accent (which is pretty good now...) and which they do quite often. I feel very accepted when my friends compliment me on how well I do, or on how I've improved (language-wise). My American friends always invite me to their parties, but I kind of take it for granted. I mean, I would do the same thing, so I don't consider it a sign of acceptance.

> I don't really have a best friend. I'm an individualist.

I don't really have a best friend. I'm an individualist. There was one girl who helped me a lot when I came here, and then I helped her once I picked up the language, but we don't consider ourselves best friends.

Education is very important to me and to our family. Ever since I was little, I knew that I would go to the university and major in something and then do another degree and do well in life. School has always been important, because my parents always told us that if we do well in school it's a reward for ourselves, and when we fail a test, for instance, we

punish ourselves. Personally, I'm a perfectionist and that, also with the pushing of my parents, motivated me to get straight As all my life. That's why I was completely devastated when I got lower grades when I first came to the U.S.; it was hard for me to study and do well in a different language.

My dream for the future is to be a linguist. I now speak English very well, and I also took Spanish for three years and French for one year and I love it! So, I guess my dreams for being a linguist/translator/language teacher were realized here and couldn't have been carried out as well in Israel.

I want Americans to understand that Israel is a very developed country! We're even better than them in some areas (like cell phones, computers, airplanes, and other important stuff). I want some ignorant people to stop asking "Do you ride on camels in Israel?" or "Do you have computers in Israel?" "NO, people we don't!" to the first question, and, "YES, people, we do!" to the second question.

I would advise newcomers to the U.S. to act like Americans when they are with Americans. If they are superficial, be superficial as well. If they are helping and understanding, be helping and understanding too. I personally think that American culture and behaviors are far different from Israeli ones, and I have learned that I will never get and accept the whole American culture.

To American teachers: If possible, please provide tutoring to new students because it can really accelerate the English learning of the kids. (I was never tutored, and I know what a loss it was for me.)

To immigrant parents: Be patient with your kids but never let them give up on themselves. Encourage them to continue, because eventually they'll get past their initial obstacles.

To immigrant students: Yes, it's hard in the beginning, but after three to six months a change occurs. Acceptance starts to emerge, and your whole point of view and attitude change for the better. Also, work hard, because being in a different country and having to go through that change only makes you a stronger person. It's an immeasurable asset in life!

Questions

1. What do you think of Na'ama's opinion of American culture? Take an anonymous poll of your classmates (slips of paper without names) and ask how many agree with Na'ama and how many disagree that most Americans are superficial and insincere. Then have a debate with one group defending Na'ama's position and one group defending American culture. Use concrete examples and not just opinions.

2. How did you define *superficial?* How did you define *American culture?* Take another poll after the debate and see if the results have changed.

3. Na'ama says she is an individualist and doesn't have a best friend. Do you like to be alone or do you prefer to be with friends? What are activities you like to do alone and ones you want to do with others?

4. Read the book *Abraham: A Journey to the Heart of Three Faiths* by Bruce Feiler. What are some of the relationships that tie together the three major religions in Na'ama's family's experience? In small groups, write a one-act play or make a short video about the children of Abraham.

5. Na'ama's family has lived in three countries. In Yemen, the majority of people celebrate Ramadan ending in the holiday of Eid-al-Fitr; in Israel, the majority celebrates Hanukkah; and in the U.S. the majority celebrates Christmas. All three holidays happen around the same time of year. Find out what each holiday represents and one custom observed during the holiday. If you

don't celebrate any of those holidays, explain to your classmates one holiday and custom that you do observe.

Research

* Find Israel on a map. Name the countries that surround Israel. If Na'ama is 16 and her parents are around 40 years old, let's say her grandparents are around 65. Na'ama's grandparents probably emigrated from Yemen to Israel around 1949. Research the history of Israel and try to discover how and why Na'ama's grandparents' families might have gone there around that time. See *http://www.jewishvirtuallibrary.org/jsource/vjw /Yemen.html#Ancient%20History.*

* Where is Yemen? Find out three things about Yemenite history and three things about Yemenite culture and report them back to your class.

* Malawach is a fried pizza-size pancake. The toppings vary from cinnamon and toasted nuts to sour cream, crumbles of ground beef, spicy sautéed vegetables, or even an omelet! If you want to know how to make one, go to *www.floras-hideout.com/food/break_rec.html.*

Activities

Some activities related to Na'ama's story:

Your Family's Immigration/Migration Story (in the section Immigration and Citizenship)

Public and Private Behaviors and Topics of Conversations (in the section Cultures and Customs)

Holidays and Celebrations (in the section Cultures and Customs)

Values and Behaviors (in the section Cultures and Customs)

People in Jamaica Are Very Welcoming

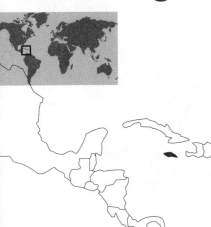

Name: Naomi

Age: 18

Home country: Jamaica

Residence in U.S.: Connecticut

My name is Naomi and I am from Jamaica. My mother's mother asked that I be named Naomi. It is a name from the Bible and in Jamaica it is thought that a child with a biblical name will grow up to be a good person. Jamaica was a colony of England from the 1600s to 1962, and most of the people in the country today are descendents of African slaves. The official language is English, but there is also a Creole-type language that people speak in Jamaica as well. It mixes English words with its own accent and grammatical system.

I was born in Kingston, which is the country's capital city. I never knew my father because he passed away before I was born. I lived in Kingston with my mother and brother until I was four months old, but I spent most of the rest of my childhood with my aunt in the countryside. My aunt took care of me because my mother worked long hours as a security guard. In my aunt's town there was always something to do and it was really pretty.

I was sort of a tomboy and loved to climb trees and always be outside playing. When I was six, I went back to Kingston and attended school there. Like kids in all schools there, we wore uniforms. Ours were purple and white.

In Jamaica, there were lots of things for kids to do. We played all sorts of ball games. One was called dandy-shandy. It was played with a short milk carton that was stuffed with papers and shaped into a ball. The game was like dodgeball—the person in the middle had to avoid getting hit by the ball, which was often thrown really hard. Another game was called Chinese skip. Two people would attach rubber bands to their feet and another person would jump over them, but then the kids with the bands would raise them higher each time and the middle person had to try to jump higher and higher to stay in the game.

Traditional foods in Jamaica include a lot of dishes with peas—sometimes called beans here—including kidney beans, gunga peas, and pigeon peas. Common meals in Jamaica include chicken or beef with rice and peas [beans]. Another favorite Jamaican dish is curried goat or chicken with rice. The food often is pretty spicy and we still make most of the same dishes here in America, but might leave out the goat curry one! Jamaica has lots of delicious fruits as well, like *ackee,* which is bright red on the outside with soft yellow fleshy fruit inside. It's hard to find it fresh in some places in the U.S., but some stores sell it in cans. Saltfish is the national dish. A common breakfast in Jamaica includes ackee and saltfish. Plantains—which are like bananas—mangoes, papayas, mammee apples, and coconuts are plentiful in Jamaica, but the stores in America don't sell some of the fruits and vegetables from Jamaica.

Christmas is a great holiday in Jamaica—a time to be with family, wish everyone a "Merry Christmas," have a big dinner, and perhaps give a present to someone special. Jamaicans also celebrate Boxing Day, the day after Christmas, with fairs and dances and family trips to the beach. It also is a time to remember other people. We did this by giving little boxes of money.

In the spring and summer, there are spectacular celebrations that are part of Jamaica Carnival. It is like Mardi Gras here in the U.S. There are huge parades, and people in colorful and wild costumes, and music and dancing. In Kingston, tens of thousands of people join the parade and festivities.

People in Jamaica are very inviting and welcoming to people of all classes and colors. I think the country is less divided than the United States. Everyone mostly feels equal there. You might say Jamaicans are mellower and more open to others. In the United States, there is more division, more exclusion, because of your income or your race.

I came to the United States when I was about 13 years old. My grandmother had come here ten years before and had filed the papers for me, my mother, and my brother to come as well. My family wanted a better life and more opportunities to succeed. But it took ten years for us to be able to come to the U.S. I wasn't really nervous about the trip, but it was my first time on a plane. Actually, I didn't know very much about the United States and I thought it would be just like Jamaica! I was very sad to leave my friends and relatives—aunts, uncles, and cousins. But my favorite aunts and uncles are here now.

I have lived in Connecticut since coming to the U.S. five years ago. I live with my mother and work with her at an agency that helps newly arrived refugees and immigrants resettle in the United States. I graduated from high school a year ago and am now in the process of trying to join the U.S. Marine Corps. My dream is to join the U.S. Marines.

I have taken preliminary tests already, and if I pass the next test I will go to basic training. For the time being, I will continue to work and if I don't join the Marines, I will save to go to college. This is a goal I hope I achieve because it will be a good challenge, very educational, and certainly exciting.

Either way, I will strive to accomplish my goals in life. It may be a challenge, but you learn a lot about competition and hard work when you are faced with tough challenges.

In addition, my faith is very important to me and brings me peace in my life. I belong to the Seventh Day Adventist Church, which I attend on Saturday, and also to the Pentecostal Church, which holds services on Sunday. Church has taught me the importance of generosity and compassion for others.

My mother felt that our education was very important. I attended school in Jamaica from age 5 until age 13, when we came to America. People have to pay for their children's uniforms, books, supplies, and lunches in Jamaica, so families had to make sacrifices to send their children to school.

The first school I attended in the U.S. was a regional vocational high school, and it was pretty hard to adjust there. Although I often keep to myself, I also consider myself a compassionate person, always try to be kind to others and be supportive. I am someone who also defends and protects people who are being picked on or left out. This first school was very difficult to adjust to; not everyone was nice and I found it hard to adjust to the cliques and all. Then I went to the public high school and things got better from then on. I think the biggest disappointment for me has been how hard it's been to find true friends. I deal with this by "dusting my feet off," being a bit more cautious, but still not being hard and bitter. I am basically an optimistic and caring person and will continue to be.

I am sort of a loner by nature, or maybe I should say just really independent—I call myself a "lone star." I didn't have a lot of trouble making friends, but was disappointed by some people I thought were friends who turned out not to be so nice, but maybe that's just junior high and high school. When I was a freshman in high school I made a really good friend and we stayed best friends for about four years. We went to the same school and we both were "lone stars," I guess. Today, I have several really close friends—they are Jamaican, so we had a lot in common right from the start. My best friend recently moved to New York and I really miss her.

I have participated in some classes and programs where I have met people from many different cultures. And I have been involved in other community activities as well because I believe that you should try and *do a good deed per day because then you know deep down you helped someone who needed it.* I just have to say, regardless of what happens, you should try to just keep your head high. Whatever the problem might be, *do not* let it get the best of you. You just have to take things one step at time and stay strong, even when the battle gets tough.

There is much more to Jamaica than reggae.

I don't think Americans know as much as they might about Jamaica and Jamaican people. Many Americans know about our music—reggae—and many really like it. Although they listen to our music, dance to it, and spend vacations in my beautiful country, a lot of people do not understand the struggle and pain of the hard life Jamaican people experience. There is much more to Jamaica than reggae. I am shocked to find racism and prejudice against Jamaicans, and even more so when it comes from people who dance to our music and visit our country.

In my opinion, you cannot help newcomers by reading or following some method you got from a book or learned in a workshop. You just have to be yourself and let things flow, and just let the words and the actions come from the heart—that's all. It's important to do fun things with new people and provide all sorts of ways for everyone (in schools, communities, and neighborhoods) to be able to do things together. That's how you get to know different kinds of people and learn to get along.

Questions

1. What do you know about Jamaican food and music? Why do you think the food and music would be popular in the United States if there is prejudice against Jamaicans?

2. Why do you think Naomi's first choice is to join the Marine Corps and only save for college if that doesn't happen?

3. What is the difference between being a "loner" and being independent? Which do you think is true of Naomi? How would you describe yourself? Why?

4. What is a *Creole language?* Find out where Creole languages are spoken besides Jamaica.

5. Try to play Chinese skip. See if you can find out why a Chinese game might be played in Jamaica.

6. What is your philosophy for overcoming challenges? How does it compare to Naomi's?

7. How do you think Naomi's religious beliefs have helped her? Can you list some religious beliefs on family values that have helped you and explain why?

8. Naomi describes disappointment in classmates who she thought were her friends. Has that ever

happened to you? What do you expect from
your friends? (See the Friendship activity.)

Research

- Look up some Jamaican recipes. Pick one and
  make it to share with friends. Be careful how
  much spice you put in it!

- Read about the colonization of Jamaica by the
  British. Find out how the British influenced the
  institutions of Jamaica, especially the type of government and the school system. How are these
  Jamaican institutions different from American
  institutions?

- Learn about the Jamaican Creole language and
  the origins of reggae music. How did reggae
  become popular outside of Jamaica? See
  http://debate.uvm.edu/dreadlibrary/
  herbold.html.

Activities

Some activities related to Naomi's story:

Friendship (in the section Cultures and Customs)

Religion (in the section Cultures and Customs)

Living in a Global World (in the section Linking the
Classroom to the Community)

Linking Newcomers to Institutions and Clubs (in
the section Linking the Classroom to the
Community)

Food Is about Unity within a Family at the Table

Name: Jennie

Age: 16

Home country: China

Residence in U.S.: West Virigina

M y Chinese name is *Mun Dee*. The English equivalent is *Mandy,* but everyone calls me Jennie. My mother named me after her father's side, in which everyone had the middle name of *Mun.* My parents originally are from Fuzhou, China. They moved to the U.S. for a better living for themselves and their future generations.

I never actually lived in China, but I did have long stays that lasted for months. At that time, my parents stayed in Hong Kong. It was always hot in the summer (with high humidity), so we mainly wore light clothes. Walking was the major means of transportation. My parents usually walked to school which, back then, could have been a couple miles.

Chinese and most Asian cultures are traditional and conservative. When it comes down to the most important value, it's about passing on the heritage to the next generation.

Food has always been important to Chinese people. To them, it's about unity within a family at the table. One tradition I remember well is having *dim sum.* Dim sum is served in the late morning, early afternoon. It's considered a lunch with dozens of delicious dishes one can pick out. Most of the food is steamed or fried.

While growing up, education has been highly stressed so we can achieve the best. My parents both have their high school education, but did not have the time or money to go to college in China. My mother had to stay home and take care of her younger brother. My father joined the navy. One of my parents' reasons for immigrating to the U.S. was to provide a better education for my brother and me. My older brother, Tony, has now graduated from DePaul University in Chicago, Illinois.

Our family lives in West Virginia where my parents own a Chinese restaurant. I'm currently a senior in high school. I'm active in many organizations, enjoying a normal teenage life. I belong to my high school's multicultural club to spread the awareness of diversity in schools. We work on such projects not only to teach about other cultures, but also to have fun at the same time. To raise funds, we have cultural fundraisers.

In high school there are so many people with different interests, it's hard not to find someone that you have something in common with. That's when I realized I was accepted in American society. Before then, I felt gawky and awkward about who I was.

I met my best friend, Jamie, in middle school. One of the reasons why I became close to her is that she is Korean. Although she was adopted, she still shares the same qualities of an Asian. She knows how Asian hair is, how dark we tend to tan, and most importantly, how we are perceived in today's society.

Chinese Americans are just like everyone else, leading everyday lives. We all don't have high IQs or know martial arts. For the record, most Chans aren't related to Jackie Chan!

I would like to pursue a degree in international studies at a prestigious university such as Stanford or Northwestern. Later, I would like to help the world by either working at the United Nations or becoming a Goodwill Ambassador. Back in China, that would be a hard goal, as not many people have the chance to go to college at all compared to the many colleges and universities in America. In China, it's like a competition. Since opportunity depends on intelligence and financial status, people with potential dreams can't always get the education they deserve.

One disappointment for me in the U.S. has been people who cheat immigrants. The smallest thing can make a difference. A good example would be a cashier overcharging someone who has just arrived here. I was hurt at how insensitive people can be, but I realized that I could speak up. Everyone in this country has a right to speak up.

I would tell new immigrant kids to have no regrets. Compared to some other times in its history, it's now a good time to immigrate to the U.S. without much hostility, as it has now become a diverse nation. The U.S. brings a lot to everyone—food, shelter, work, education, and most importantly, freedom.

American teachers should teach students about other cultures. To work with today's society, they can add a modern twist, say what a so-and-so teenager does in another country compared to us. Pen pals are also a suggestion so American kids can get to know about kids in other countries.

American parents and students should take notice of the newcomers and welcome them. When I was in school, I was usually the only one of Chinese descent. By learning about my culture with more consideration, they can understand where people like me come from. Also, communication is the key to support. By not befriending a newcomer, you may never know who this person truly is except by assumptions (that are usually false).

> Just because they are newcomers doesn't mean that they don't know anything.

One piece of advice to new Chinese immigrants is to take in everything. You can still practice your same culture, but you also must realize you are on U.S. soil...there's millions of other cultures. New immigrants need to be open-minded and understanding. They should also know that their word matters. Just because they are newcomers doesn't mean that they don't know anything.

Questions

1. Where is Fuzhou, China? How far is Fuzhou from Hong Kong?

2. What would you say is the most important value in your culture and why? How does your opinion compare with that of other students in your class?

3. Do you have stereotypes about Chinese people? Are they any of the ones mentioned by Jennie? Have you met a Chinese student who does not fit those stereotypes?

4. Do you have a multicultural or international club in your school? What kinds of activities do they sponsor? What foreign languages are taught at your school? Do you have a global studies course? Why would or wouldn't you participate in these clubs/courses?

5. If you are or you know a young person who was adopted by a family or parent of a different culture than his/her own, see if you can have a conversation with him/her about the advantages and challenges of growing up in a multicultural home.

6. Tell your classmates about a time when you realized someone was cheating you or someone else. Why did this happen? What did you do? What, if anything, do you wish you had done differently and why?

7. Why does Jennie say our assumptions about a newcomer are usually false? What can we do about that?

Research

- The Port of Fuzhou is a "sister city" to the Port of Tacoma, Washington in the U.S. Find out more about the Sister Cities Program at the website below and see if your city or one near you has a "sister" in another country. See *http://www.porto ftacoma.com/aboutus.cfm?sub-38&lsub-97*.

- Find out exactly what is included in a dim sum lunch. Go to a Chinese restaurant and order it or look up a recipe and try to make one of the dishes. Here are two websites to help you: a dim sum menu at *www.dimsum.com/ds1.html* and a dim sum China curriculum unit at *www.new ton.mec.edu/Angier/DimSum/DimSum%20T.of Con.HomePg.html*.

Activities

Some activities related to Jennie's story:

- Family Rules (in the section Cultures and Customs)

- Welcoming Activities (in the section Linking the Classroom to the Community)

- What We Learn from the Media (in the section Stereotypes, Tolerance, and Diversity)

- Foods (in the section Cultures and Customs)

My Father Had All the Authority in the House

Name: Ramon

Age: 18

Home country: Mexico

Residence in U.S.: North Carolina

I was named after my grandmother Ramona. It's a popular and typical name in Mexico. Culture-wise, in my family the kids are named after parents and grandparents. Part of my heritage is being named after my grandmother.

I am from a town in the state of Jalisco in northern Mexico. Every year we spent two weeks celebrating the *Virgen Santa Isabel de Quililla* during December. The first week we would get up early every day (6:00 A.M.) to sing to the Virgin, do the rosary, and go to mass around 11:00 A.M. Then everyone met in the town square to chat and have fun.

The second week of the celebration was the same in the mornings, but in the afternoons there was dancing and music, and three days of rodeo. We had a big celebration on the last day to select the queen and princess of the town. On the last day during the rodeo there would be a speech and then the party would start. There was bull riding, horses,

and music all day. The band came later to the party
and everyone went to the town square to have fun.

After the mass each day, a sponsoring family
would invite the town to their house to have food.
Some maybe couldn't serve a full lunch, but they
had at least coffee and bread and cookies.

The festival showed me how the town came
together at that time. Maybe families or people
were angry at each other for something, but they
still would celebrate with each other. I grew up seeing how my own family came together and it really
affected me. I can't wait to go back to my hometown in December if I can save the money. It will
be my first time back in six years.

My father was the first in our family to come to
the U.S. He and my uncle were farmworkers in
Southern California. They picked strawberries and
lettuce. He sent us money but it wasn't enough. In
Mexico my father had animals, corn, and other
crops, but when he moved we didn't have those
any more. I stayed with my grandparents in Mexico
for three years while my two older brothers
worked with my dad in California to make more
money to send to us.

Eventually, my whole family moved to the U.S.
because Dad thought it would be easier to support
us and we would have more opportunities. We
came in pairs: first my mom and my sister, then my
two older brothers, and then me and my other
brother.

My father lived in California for 15 or 20 years
total. I lived there for seven years. While I was there
I went to elementary and middle school and started
high school. In California there were bilingual
classes. I had trouble learning English but had lots
of help.

After that we moved to North Carolina. First we
lived with an aunt and uncle for a couple of months

while my mom and dad found jobs to pay the rent. Then we rented a house for a year. Then my parents bought a house and we're living there now.

I got in the Migrant Education Program and finished high school in North Carolina. There were many Spanish-speaking people in L.A., but in North Carolina there are fewer Hispanics and more students straight from Mexico and other countries who are learning English. North Carolina newcomers have problems with English and in getting along with others. I decided to help out and started getting involved with tutoring and the AIM (migrant student) club.

Neither of my parents and none of my older brothers graduated from high school, and college is new for them. I know they feel proud of me; they've said it before. They've said just ask for anything and they'll give it.

I am getting financial aid at school. I told my mom what the costs would be otherwise and she said they never could pay that. I realize how important it is to find ways to pay for it. I feel more support sometimes from my mom. My father never showed much support, but I never talked to him about it, never showed him what I was doing in school. I know my father cares, but when it comes to education, he doesn't know how it's affecting me. I know I have my parents' support though, and my brothers' too. When I graduated from high school, my brothers and sisters congratulated me for being the first. My younger siblings look up to me, and I am encouraging them to get an education. I feel really proud of my family's support, however they can do it, and I appreciate it.

My roommate is my best friend right now. He was born in Houston, but his family is from Veracruz, Mexico. We met in high school—he was one of the first people I met there. We thought it was funny that we were both Mexicans and in Spanish class together. I had friends from other places, and with him there are some cultural differences, but it's comfortable because we have a lot of similarities. He really helped me a lot, since he graduated one year ahead of me. I was slacking off as a senior and he told me I had to work hard—he was really supportive. When I decided to go to this university, he withdrew from his school to go here, too.

We get along good, it's really comfortable. If it was someone else I couldn't do stuff like the things I do at home with my family. We have some of the same traditions like at home. For example, we listen to the same music, watch *novellas* [soap operas], and have the same interests. We bring food from home and share it. That's also why we get along, because we share everything.

Right now, I'm trying to do the SAF [Student Action with Farmworkers] internship. At school I'm interested in anthropology, ethnography, different cultures. I'm part of the LASO [Latin American Student Organization] club, which has a bunch of students from different countries in Latin America. I'm involved in the Multicultural Center, and I know the coordinator really well. In September, I sat on a panel at the University Center that was about different cultures in Latin American countries. They also had African American and Asian panels—it was pretty fun to be involved with, to learn and ask questions. It's a fun way to learn about other cultures.

The hardest time for me was when I first moved to North Carolina. In California I had a lot of Hispanic friends and didn't feel that left out. In North Carolina, I experienced a different culture, one that only spoke English and was really different. So I'd try to find solutions, ask for help. Basically, I wouldn't stop trying, trying to find help. If there was a big problem, I would try to solve everything with words. I wouldn't get mad or disappointed. I would try to find a solution. If I ever gave up, I knew the rest of my life I'd think about what I could have done to change my situation.

When I was back in California, I had a heavy accent and people made fun of me. I came to realize it wasn't because they were mean or could speak better than me. They had the same problems in class. I didn't want to read in class, and in North Carolina it was the same. Once in North Carolina a teacher made me read out loud. My accent was a little heavy. I expected people to laugh but after I read no one said anything, and the teacher said "Good job." In California I would usually hear someone laugh, and at first it made me insecure. The first time I read out loud in North Carolina made me feel accepted.

People here say we Mexicans drink too much, are lazy, and are taking all the jobs. But we just came for opportunities. Anyone in our position would do this, try to improve ourselves, go to school, to do whatever we want to do. There are a lot of barriers stopping us from trying to improve ourselves. We don't come to take up space and jobs, and to drink. We just want opportunities that we don't have in our countries. Everyone in the U.S. has the same opportunities, but we work harder for them.

I've already realized one dream that I couldn't have achieved in Mexico: finishing high school. I wouldn't have had the support. My town in Mexico only had an elementary school; the closest middle school was one hour away. I don't remember anyone going there. People weren't encouraged to go to school, but to work instead.

I don't know what I want to do, but I would like to get involved in anthropology and archaeology, studying cultures from the past. There's not much opportunity for that in Mexico. If I still lived there, I would probably be working, taking care of animals and the land. I've seen it with my cousins and

uncles who are still there. I'm going to school to get
a career.

Where I grew up, my father had all the authority
in the house. My older brothers would go to school
until May or June. If my father needed them to work
in the fields with animals or corn, he had the
authority to do what he thought was best. In the
U.S., parents encourage kids to go to school and do
activities. My older brothers would go to do activities like sports when they were young. My father
wouldn't encourage or even allow this. I remember
my dad punishing my older brother for sneaking
out to play soccer.

My father has changed a lot; I can see the difference. Now he encourages us to go to school and to
get involved in activities. He kind of regrets how he
was before. He encourages my younger brothers to
do their homework and that surprises me. I'm not
used to seeing parents so involved in school, talking
with teachers about how their kids can improve.

I think parents should be involved in school.
Parents should meet teachers and their kids' classmates and try to get involved with other families.
Kids should get involved in school activities, clubs,
and sports. First I wasn't involved; when I started
playing soccer and joining clubs I felt more
involved and closer to the American experience. I
encourage this—it makes you feel a part of things; it
makes you feel good.

Some people think a language barrier means you
don't know anything or can't do stuff an English
speaker can. I helped a friend who couldn't speak
English at all, but he could do well in algebra
(because you don't need English for it). In other
classes, students and teachers wouldn't help him
out and didn't think he could improve. Once I
helped translate an English assignment for him and
he really impressed the teacher with his work.

> **Understand that
> it's hard to learn
> a new language
> and culture.**

I would like Americans not to think newcomers can't do anything. Understand that it's hard to learn a new language and culture. Immigrants can do stuff; they're not ignorant. Don't be prejudiced; try to work with them any way you can.

Questions

1. What five states in the U.S. used to belong to Mexico? (See *www.historyguy.com/Mexican-American_War.html*)? How many states are there in Mexico now? Find the state of Jalisco on a map. How far is it from the U.S. border? Trace a route you might take to get from the capital of Jalisco to Los Angeles.

2. What do you think happened to the animals and crops that Ramon's father used to own in Mexico? Why?

3. What are *anthropology* and *archaeology?* Why do you think Ramon might be interested in studying cultures from the past? What famous archaeological sites exist in Mexico?

4. Ramon was the first in his family to finish high school. Are you the first in your family to do something—to play an instrument, to win an award, to publish a poem or story? How did your family react to your accomplishment?

5. Do you have younger siblings who look up to you? Or did you look up to older brothers and sisters? Why? How has that affected your life?

6. Ramon said his father has changed his mind about education. Why do you think that has happened? Do you know an adult who has changed his or her mind about something important to you? Why did the change occur?

7. Have you ever faced a big challenge that made you mad or disappointed, like Ramon? If so, what did you do to overcome it?

8. What is the difference between bilingual education and ESL? Hold a debate in your class on this topic, including the advantages and disadvantages of each approach in terms of their objectives, methods, costs, and results.

Research

● Who was Cesar Chavez? See *www.sfsu.edu/~cecipp/ cesar_ chavez/chavezhome.htm.*

● Look through the Student Action with Farmworkers (SAF) website at *http://cds.aas. duke.edu/saf/mission.htm.* Then read the SAF fact sheet on farmworkers at *http://cds.aas.duke. edu/saf/pdfs/fwfactsheet.pdf.* Find three facts you didn't know and share them with a partner in pairs. Make your own fact sheet on a culture or group of your choice and share it with your class.

Activities

Some activities related to Ramon's story:

Family Rules (in the section Cultures and Customs)

Who Is Coming to the U.S. now? (in the section Immigration and Citizenship)

Myths and Facts about Immigrants (in the section Immigration and Citizenship)

I Dream to Become a Migrant Lawyer

Name: Noemy

Age: 16

Home country: Mexico

Residence in U.S.: North Carolina

My name, Noemy, is in the Bible. My mother heard of it and named me that. It means "delightful and pleasant," and that's how I truly am. I am from Jalisco state, in Mexico.

A tradition that we have in Mexico that is meaningful for me is celebrating the *Quinceanera*. That's when a girl in Mexico turns *quince años,* fifteen years old. She has a big party, and she wears a big pretty dress that makes her look like a princess. It's a very special day because it is like a celebration, celebrating her change from a girl to a young lady. We celebrate that a girl at 15 is now going to a new phase of life where she needs to think more like an adult and be more mature. In the United States people don't celebrate that day; they don't think that being 15 is anything important.

Another tradition we have in Mexico is for all the family and close friends to gather for Christmas and eat a big dinner together. We also celebrate the day of Our Lady of Guadalupe every 12th of December. We have a big mass in memory of Our Lady of

Guadalupe. On every 6th of January, we eat a piece
of a pie. Inside the pie there is a little baby toy, and
whoever gets that baby toy in their slice of pie has
to plan a party remembering the birth of Jesus.

My family moved to the U.S. to get better lives
and a better education. When I first got to the
United States, I lived in California. After eight years
my parents saw that we needed better opportunities for job resources so we moved to North
Carolina. We needed to start all over because it was
a big change moving from one state to another, not
knowing what to expect. We first lived in my aunt's
house for two months. Then we found our own
house and have been living there for more than half
a year.

My family thinks education plays a big part of success in life. My dad is the kind of man who doesn't
get involved in his kids' education, because all he
thinks he has to do is to bring the money and food
to the family.

On the other hand, my mom was always there for
me. Even if she didn't understand the material, she
made sure I did my homework. It was really difficult
for her to help me after the sixth grade because
that was the last grade she had completed. She has
been involved a lot in my education ever since elementary school. She was at my fifth grade
graduation and my middle school graduation.
Hopefully she will be at my high school and college
graduations too. My mother expects a lot from me.
She really wants me to be someone in life and earn
good money. She doesn't want me to be stuck in a
factory earning minimum wage.

I remember the moment I experienced that made
me feel accepted by my American friends and
teachers. It happened after I took a summer enrich-
ment class in chemistry. The following fall I was
able to answer a question that no one else knew in
my chemistry class.

> **It is not what everybody else thinks of people but what I find out for myself.**

My best friend is Maday. We were in an accounting class and I noticed she needed help with English and the material. I asked her if I could help her and she said sure. Since then we have become good friends. I think what is important for understanding among different cultures is building friendships and being aware that it is not what everybody else thinks of people but what I find out for myself.

I dream to become a migrant lawyer, and help other people that need my help. My dream would have been hard to realize in Mexico because I wouldn't have the same opportunities as I do here. In the U.S. it would be easier and faster for me to make my dream come true.

I would like Americans to know that Mexicans are not only short and dark skinned with brown eyes. Some of us are tall, light skinned, with blue or green eyes.

I would suggest to new U.S. resident children to learn the English language as soon as possible so that everything here will be easier for them. I would suggest to new U.S. resident parents to support their children in anything at school so that they can help them become someone in life.

I would suggest to teachers to have patience with their newly arrived students and recognize what the students do know instead of what they don't know.

Questions

1. Noemy is Ramon's sister. (If you haven't read it yet, read Ramon's story now.) Compare their stories and see what is similar and what is different about them. Interview your brother, sister, or cousin about your family history and have him

or her do the same with you. Why do you think some memories and feelings are the same and some so different when people are from the same family?

2. Have you ever moved from one country or one state to another? Why did you do that and how did you feel about it? How did you get accepted in your new environment?

3. Have you had a parent or other adult encourage you to improve—maybe your schoolwork, or sports or music skills—even if they couldn't do it themselves? Did their encouragement help you? Why or why not?

4. Noemy became friends with someone she helped in school. How have you made friends? Do you and your friends help each other? How?

5. Noemy's mother wants her to be able to "earn good money." Do this activity to find out why. What is the current *minimum wage* in the U.S.? See *http://www.dol.gov/esa/minwage/america.htm*. Multiply that hourly wage times 160 hours per month (40 hour workweek x 4 weeks per month). Find out the average of how much your family spends on food each month and what a two-bedroom apartment costs to rent per month in your neighborhood. Add those two costs together and subtract them from the total you got above for one month's work at minimum wage. How much do you have left to spend on parties, clothes, books, a car, and so on?

6. Do you remember a time when you felt really good because of something you knew or could do, like Noemy's experience in chemistry class? Close your eyes and try to picture your experience. Has that experience influenced you in any way? If so, how?

Research

- See how a couple of middle school girls describe the Quinceanera at *www.hpl.lib.tx.us/youth /cinco_quince.html.* How does the girl in the photo on the website compare with Noemy's descriptions of Mexicans? How is the Quinceanera the same or different from a Sweet 16 party? What, if any, is a similar celebration for boys? What do you think it really means for a girl to "become a woman" or a boy to "become a man?"

- What does Noemy mean when she says her dream is to become a migrant lawyer? Look at the certificate program in immigration law on the website *www.tsu.edu/academics/law/pro-grams/immigration/index.asp* and see the types of courses she might have to take. Try to imagine what her job would be like. What is your dream career and why do you want to pursue it?

Activities

Some activities related to Noemy's story:

Friendship (in the section Cultures and Customs)

Schools (in the section Cultures and Customs)

Holidays and Celebrations (in the section Cultures and Customs)

I Started Fasting When I Was 10 Years Old

Name: Adib

Age: 13

Home country: Iraq

Residence in U.S.: Virginia

My name is Adib, the name of my father's brother. One translation for my name from our dialect of Arabic means "the writer." I was born in a holy city in southern Iraq. We moved to Lebanon in 1998 because of political tensions and the war. My mother is from Lebanon. We have relatives there who helped us as we prepared to travel to the West.

Our family is Shiite Muslim. My favorite holiday is Ramadan, especially Eid-al-Fitr, when we have a party which officially ends the fasting that we do for a month before that. I started fasting when I was about 10 years old—that's the normal age to start. For Eid-al-Fitr in Iraq, my family and I would usually go to a relative's house and have a huge meal and party with family and friends. My mom says she noticed that in the U.S. you don't have as many relatives living with you, like uncles, aunts, cousins, and grandparents, as we do in Iraq and Lebanon.

Another thing about life in Iraq and Lebanon that is different from the States is that there are more

classes in school and the curriculum is harder there, especially in math. Also, children and teens have to be more polite than American kids are to adults. I think that's a good thing. When you talk to your teacher or when you are called on in class, students must first stand and then ask or respond to a question.

After living in Lebanon for five years, my parents, my younger sister, and I moved to the U.S. last year so we children could get a better educational opportunity. I love our city in Virginia! I'm in the in eighth grade now and I like school. I just went on a field trip to Washington, D.C. with my class two weeks ago. My favorite thing was the tour of the Air and Space Museum.

Both my father and my mother graduated from college. My dad has a degree in chemistry. My mom has a degree in agricultural science and used to work as a teacher. My family expects me to go to college, but I don't know what I want to do after that. I'm pretty good in English. I started out last year in ESL classes and this year I am in honors English. I scored 4.5 out of 5 on my proficiency exam and I have straight As.

ESL classes were very helpful in getting to know different cultures. So was taking French for a semester. My ESL teacher hosted an "International Night" for the school, and students and their families brought different foods, music, and clothing. That was a nice way to see how many cultures there were at my school.

I have many friends here but at least two I'd call "best friends." Their names are Patrick and Daniel. I met Patrick in class and we became good friends. I made a lot of friends playing soccer—I met Daniel playing indoor soccer. Soccer was a big activity that opened the door for me to meet other kids.

I dream about being a soccer player in the Brazilian or Italian league. If I have to choose some-

> **ESL classes were very helpful in getting to know different cultures.**

thing academic, I would want to be an engineer who works on planes or maybe with technology and computers. There is not much money where I used to live for higher education, and very few scholarships, so I have a better chance of doing that here. I just earned a full scholarship to attend a private school in Virginia. That probably wouldn't have happened in Iraq or Lebanon.

I feel pretty accepted in the U.S. There wasn't really any "moment" that made me feel that way or any huge obstacle to overcome. One big problem I had, though, was that some of the kids in my class had stereotypes about the Middle East. One boy said he thought that no women in the Middle East drive cars and that most people are "poor," or that there is "war everywhere." My teacher didn't even correct the boy because she didn't know what the Middle East is like either.

A small problem was U.S. history class. I suffered through my first year of that. It was really difficult to understand it because I didn't know anything about the subject. To overcome this, I studied very hard. What was even harder to understand was that after studying so much about American history and a little about Europe, we only had three weeks to study the entire rest of the world!

I think getting parents involved in their children's education is very important for kids who are new to the U.S. Having meetings with both the student and their parents helps everyone to figure out where the student might be having trouble, like in U.S. history or in making friends. That kind of meeting helps you and your family and your teachers to make this situation better at home and at school.

Kids who are new to the U.S. should play sports to meet new people. They should make an effort to be social and talk with people in their classes. This is hard at first. I went to an ESL camp when I first arrived, and that's where I first made some friends and started to talk to other kids in my new environment. The camp experience helped me later to know how to fit into my new school and social life.

I want Americans to know that the Middle East is not all poor, and some parts and people are pretty rich. Some of my classmates think that people in Middle Eastern countries live in small shacks. I tell them most of the houses are bigger than the houses here in the U.S.

I think people shouldn't judge others until they can know their full story, rather than base their judgments on TV stereotypes or things they hear from people who don't know the real situation.

Questions

1. On a map, see if you can imagine the route that Adib's family might have taken if they went overland from southern Iraq to Beirut, Lebanon.

2. Do you have any relatives living with you other than your parents and siblings? Why or why not?

3. Describe some rituals or celebrations that your family does at particular times during the year. Try to find out the origin and meaning of those rituals and celebrations.

4. How many weeks, months, or classes does your school have on U.S. history and how many on the history of other countries? Why do you think that is the case?

5. What impressions do you have of Iraq and other countries in the Middle East? Where did you get those impressions? How can you find out the "real situation?"

Research

- What is a *holy city?* Where are the holy cities for Muslims in Iraq?

- What is a *Shiite Muslim?* What are the other sects of Islam? What are some differences in their beliefs and practices?

- What is *Ramadan?* Do some research on Ramadan and the festival of Eid-al-Fitr. Find out what they mean in English and how, why, and in what countries Muslims observe/celebrate those days. (For example, Adib says they fast for a month. Does that mean they don't eat for a month?) You can start with the website *www.funsocialstudies.learninghaven.com/ articles/eid.htm.*

Activities

Some activities related to Adib's story:

Religion (in the section Cultures and Customs)

What Are Stereotypes and Why Do We Use Them? (in the section Stereotypes, Tolerance, and Diversity)

What We Learn from the Media (in the section Stereotypes, Tolerance, and Diversity)

Linking Newcomers to Institutions and Clubs (in the section Linking the Classroom to the Community)

Punishment Was Getting Hit on the Hand with a Ruler

Name: Pushpanjali

Age: 18

Home country: Nepal

Residence in U.S.: Virginia

Pushpanjali is a Hindi name meaning "prayer flower." It was shortened to Pushpa when I went to school.

I was born in Katmandu, the capital of Nepal. I lived most of my first nine years with only my mother, because my father worked for an American family who lived in various countries. My father was able to come to visit every few months.

We start school very early in Nepal; I started going to school all day at age three. My parents wanted me to get a good education and I always attended private schools. We wore uniforms (a skirt, blouse, long socks up to our knees, a tie, and a belt with the school name on it), and discipline was very strict. Punishment was getting hit on the hand with a ruler…a few hits for not listening, not raising your hand to answer questions, not standing up when the teacher walked in. Punishment for more serious offenses, such as not doing homework for the week, was more severe, and in addition to more strikes on the hand, you would have to stand facing the class throughout the day. It was really humiliating.

I attended an English boarding school for several years, one year as a boarding student. We had to speak English all the time or be punished. The school had about 400 students and went through 10th grade, which is the grade you earn a School Leaving Certificate in the English system.

My family moved to the U.S. when I was nine years old. I remember being struck by how many cars and few people were on the streets. The trees and flowers around people's houses in the U.S. were also very new for me. Where I lived in Katmandu, there were very narrow streets, lots of buildings and temples, and people walked or rode bicycles.

When we arrived, we stayed with an American family who had lived in Nepal. After a month we moved to an apartment and I began elementary school. Because our school year is different (we have vacation in winter), I was put back a year. I knew English very well but didn't feel like I could speak fluently. The first year I was very quiet; I just read books all the time.

School was very different here than at home. There was no corporal punishment, no uniforms, and things seemed much more casual (we didn't stand up for the teachers). I knew most of the subjects except fractions. I hadn't studied fractions in Nepal!

At the end of the school year I made a friend. We had reading discussion groups, and one day a girl named Alison talked about a particular kind of rock. I knew about those rocks, so I talked to her! We became best friends, and she still is a friend of mine even though we don't go to the same school. Her mother was very open and warm, and she would come to my house and take me to their house. She met my parents and our parents became friends,

> My advice to new immigrants is: Don't assimilate too much; it's nice to be unique.

too. Sometimes our families would do things
together. I loved being at Alison's house. We talked
and played and her mother cooked for us.

Once I had a friend to talk to, my English became
much better and I had confidence to speak. Then
everything became easier for me.

I missed my family and friends in Nepal the first
year, especially my grandparents, uncles, and
cousins. Whenever we celebrated holidays (many
were Hindi celebrations and birthdays), I missed my
extended family because we would always get
together and have a big feast. We would wear traditional clothes and do traditional dances. The adults
would give us presents—presents were always
money. We never bought special gifts and wrapping
paper. I always used my money to buy a special
Nepali treat, a type of sour-spicy snack.

In the U.S. my family still celebrated our holidays,
but it was different without our relatives. After
awhile we met other Nepalese and we celebrated
together. A big holiday for us is *Diwali,* a festival of
lights when we light oil lamps.

When I made a Pakistani friend, it was nice to be
able to talk about things our cultures share in common that Americans do not understand.

People think I am Indian. Most don't even know
where Nepal is. I don't really care, as I like to
explain about my country. Some people say I do
well in science and math because "Indians are supposed to be good in those areas." I really don't think
I'm so good at math!

My family's expectations are that education will
make my life better; they did not have a chance to
be educated. That's why we came to the U.S.: to
give me better opportunities. And they thought it
would be easier on me if we moved when I was
young. (I have a younger sister who was born in the
U.S.) I don't recall my parents talking about educa-

tion so much…it is just really clear how important it is.

I am active in lots of things. I've played violin since the fourth grade in the school orchestra. I've been on soccer teams and played in the youth soccer league, and I also played volleyball until it took too much time after school. I've been in debate and participated in Model UN.

I'm very interested in community service. I am president of the Key Club, which has 80 members at our school. It is part of an international Kiwanis organization. There are four seasons of service, and we have to do a project each season. I am interested in health, and one season we raised money for measles vaccines for children in Africa. I thought that was really worthwhile.

I am also a Red Cross youth volunteer, which is really neat because there are many self-study units, and after you learn something well you have an opportunity to teach it to younger children. I learned about water safety and taught it at an elementary school.

I would love to be a Peace Corps volunteer someday and go back to Nepal and help my country.

When asked what I want to do, I always say, "I want to be a doctor." I don't know why; I think it's what my parents want me to say though I don't remember them telling me that! Their idea is that I would set up a practice and see patients. That's what I would have done in Nepal. I am really interested in medicine, but I think I am more interested in diseases and research related to curing diseases. I had hoped to be selected for a special summer scholarship called the Governor's School and study medicine at a university. I wasn't selected because they only took older students for the medical program, but I was awarded a scholarship to study agriculture and plants, and that was great fun and interesting, too. I made some friends through that experience and we still stay in contact.

I also like to write. I write stories all the time. When I was in the sixth grade I won an award for my story "The Magic Bead," which was published in a small journal.

I got very interested in government through a great teacher I had in AP government in the 10th grade. It was a very hard course; we had to study current events thoroughly and debate the various points of view. That really got me started watching the news.

I am now in an International Baccalaureate program in my high school. It is very challenging, as we have coursework and papers, and 150 hours of community service in the areas of action, creativity, and service. I am doing my extended essay for the year on the Manhattan Project because I learned that the person behind the key letter to the president was not Einstein; the research has been very interesting.

I guess you could say I like everything!

My advice to new immigrants is: Don't assimilate too much; it's nice to be unique. When I was younger, my parents wanted me to wear my traditional clothes or a tika (a mark on the forehead) to school on holidays, but I didn't want to. I wish I had as then people would have asked questions and I could have taught them about my country and religion.

Questions

1. If you do something wrong in class or at your school, what happens? How does the way students are disciplined reflect the values of the school, community, and culture?

2. Have your parents ever become friends with the parents of one of your friends? How and why did that happen/not happen?

3. What is a *positive stereotype?* Can you find one in Pushpa's story? How does the stereotype affect Pushpa? How would it affect you?

4. Was anyone in your family (or a friend's family) born in a different country from the rest of the family? Does that person act differently than the rest of the family in any way? How?

5. How did you meet your best friend? What things do you like to do together?

6. Have you ever had the opportunity to visit the home of a classmate or community member from another culture? If so, how was it different from your own—in terms of how rooms were used, the types and arrangement of furniture, and areas where visitors were allowed? (See the activity Public and Private Behaviors and Topics of Conversation below.)

Research

• Look up the websites of one or more of the organizations or activities in which Pushpa is involved and see if you'd like to get involved in that as well!

  www.peacecorps.gov

  www.un.org

  www.redcross.org

  www.kiwanis.org

• Pushpa's suggestions for research projects are:

  Learn about current politics in Nepal. The massacre of our royal family has made changes take place.

Research the Hindu religion, calendar, rituals, and holidays. It is a way of life.

Find Katmandu, Nepal on a map. Look at pictures to see how beautiful Nepal is. It is more than just spectacular mountains; it is green and lush like Ireland.

Activities

Some activities related to Pushpa's story:

Public and Private Behaviors and Topics of Conversation (in the section Cultures and Customs)

Family Rules (in the section Cultures and Customs)

Service Learning (in the section Linking the Classroom to the Community)

You Are Scared All the Time

Name: Liban

Age: 15

Home country: Somalia

Residence in U.S.: Minnesota

My name is Liban. My grandmother named me. I don't think there was too much meaning behind my name and it's not typical for grandmothers to name grandchildren in our country. My parents just couldn't think of a name and my grandmother suggested Liban.

We moved to the U.S. to have a better life. We wanted to get away from wars and stuff, to get a good education for me and my sister, and to just be free to be ourselves. You can do whatever you want here as long as you don't interfere with anyone or break the laws. I was young when I came and I just followed the crowd.

Since the day I was born, there was war going on in Somalia, so it was hard to see what values people had. I have forgotten about the lifestyle back there to some degree because it was a time of war and people's lives were affected by that. In the U.S. most people go to a mall, a movie, or play with friends. In Somalia most people just go to friends' houses.

I was born in Somalia. Some people say, "Somalia? Where is that?" Most people ask what language I speak. We don't have the same food as Americans. We may have the same clothing but we have different styles and looks. People should know that every country is different.

I lived in Somalia until I was six years old; then we moved to Kenya for about a year. After that, I moved to the States with my mom, my dad, and my sister. My grandmother came later.

The lifestyle in Somalia was way different from here. Back there, night and day you hear gunshots and stuff—it's scary—you can't sleep or just relax—you are scared all the time and you never know when something bad will come up. There were a couple of houses that were blown up for no reason. During war, anyone in between is in danger. I still don't know why they were fighting.

I lived in Mogadishu, the capital. I went to an Islamic school to study the Quran. We owned our own houses—my uncle lived in one place, my grandma lived in one place, and we could just go wherever we wanted. There is no bus transportation so everyone walked. We also used horses, donkeys, and stuff like that. People have cars, but what are you going to do with a car? Everyone is close by—the store is your neighbor, your uncle is your neighbor.

The main holiday in Somalia is Eid, after Ramadan. Most people think Ramadan is the holiday but it is not. After the last day of Ramadan, the next day is Eid-al-Fitr. During the Eid you eat sweets—it doesn't matter what kind of sweets. We also eat *sambousa*—it is a traditional food to eat at Ramadan time. Sambousa is made of flour formed in a triangular shape and fried. Inside are vegetables or meat or hot peppers. You eat it with good hot tea. I drank tea there all the time—but now I learned to drink coffee.

Most kids younger than me like Eid so they can't wait for it. For older people, they go and pray and sit down and talk. Kids just go and have fun. There are differences between how Eid is celebrated in Somalia and here in the U.S.

There is nothing that I could do in Somalia that I can't do here. Here in the U.S. I go to movies and play football and basketball. They do have basketball in Somalia, but the floor is sand so the ball won't bounce. Back there we don't have rims and all that stuff—you tape up a bucket or something. Soccer is really popular is Somalia.

My goals are not the same as when I lived in Somalia because it was not independent since the war. Forget about school—there was no school. Coming to the U.S. has provided us with an opportunity for education. This is one main reason my family came here to the U.S.—so we could do better with our lives.

Now I live in Minnesota where I am a freshman in high school. My favorite subjects are lunch (LOL!) and gym. I also like math. I am thinking of joining sports teams at school next year—possibly football and basketball.

Education is everything…this is what I not only have been taught by my family but it is what I have seen. Without education, you are stuck and you cannot take a step forward. School is school; no matter where you are, you learn something.

I learned English real fast by listening and trying to pick it up. Language is easier to learn when you're younger. When you are learning the language, there are some things you can't say. Like if you need help from the teacher, you can say, "Please help me," but you can't really explain what you need or want. That was hard, but I was not treated differently than other kids. When you are

> Without education, you are stuck and you cannot take a step forward.

learning the language, that is the biggest challenge—it is like you're deaf or really worse than being deaf. Body communication can also help.

I fit anywhere I go. I am talkative so I talk to everyone—I don't care who they are. I tell jokes and laugh with people. Just talk to people—that is the only way you can make friends. That is what I did. I have all kinds of friends from all different places. I don't use the phrase *best friend*—I use *friends*. Best friends can start a fight. ("I thought *I* was your best friend." "Okay, you both are!")

You also need to get involved. I live in a large apartment complex—there are people from many different ethnic groups and backgrounds living there. I am involved in a youth program for boys in my building. We get together with a few college student volunteers and play sports, games, hang out, etc.

The Neighborhood Reinvestment Corporation (NRIC) group is trying to develop the concept of a block club in my apartment building, but instead of a block club they are developing "floor clubs." I am the youth leader for that; I represent the people my age and explain the things we don't like and what we want. The group tries to bring community and peace back to the neighborhood. It involves people from different cultural groups who live in the building.

Here is my advice to kids who come to the U.S.:

1. Be yourself—that is the main thing.

2. Don't put yourself down and don't let any body put you down.

3. Work hard.

4. Don't take yourself out of the picture. If you are in the classroom, don't just sit in the corner quietly. You have to show the

teacher and the people in the classroom that you are there. Just communicate—that is number one.

5. Ask for help if you need it; say what you want to say (other than bad words).

I suggest that American teachers have someone in the classroom who speaks the same language as the newcomer (and also English)...to be an interpreter between them. All I know is that I never had that. I learned it on my own; I did not have any other Somali kids in class throughout grade school.

To American kids: Don't make fun of them [kids from other countries]. If you go to another country, you won't speak their language. Help them if you can and if you can't, just leave them alone.

I suggest to parents that they offer to help with homework; ask their children what they learned and review it with them. For children, have your own parents speak to you in English as much as they can.

My parents have good English abilities; of my friends, three out of four have parents with English language difficulties—that is what most of the kids have problems with...they can't get help from home with homework, reading, and writing.

One thing my mom told me was grab a book and just write whatever you see...copy out of the book, so your handwriting will get better—this helped me a lot. Writing in cursive was the hardest thing I have ever done.

I am not a future guy—I am a present-and-two-years-from-now guy. I plan to graduate from high school—that is number one on my list—with a good GPA. Then I plan to go to college, of course. I don't know yet what I want to major in because that is too far ahead in the future.

Questions

1. Discuss in trios or small groups what you think Liban means when he says "There was war going on so it was hard to see what values people had." Why do you think people's values change in times of war? What are your values? Do you think they would change if you were in a place that was at war? How? Why? Report out loud to your class.

2. What is an Islamic school? What is the Quran (Koran)? Why does Liban say "there was no school" if he attended this type of school?

3. Liban says he can fit in anywhere because he is talkative and talks to everyone. Are you the same? What is your reaction to new people?

4. What does Liban mean by "body communication?" In pairs, try to ask your classmate for something you need without speaking any words. Did he or she understand? Why or why not?

5. What is *cursive writing?* Why do you think learning to write that way was the hardest thing Liban had ever done?

6. Liban has five pieces of advice for new kids to the U.S. With your friends or class, discuss those five ideas. Do you think they are good ones for American kids too? Why or why not?

7. What do you think of Liban's statement that he can only think two years into the future? Can you think of anything in Liban's past that might influence that? What about you? Do you know what you want to do in the future? Why or why not?

8. Have you ever tasted food seasoned with cumin or cardamom? With an adult near you, make sambousas using the recipe below. Try to find in

what countries other than Somalia the people eat sambousas.

Sambousas

This is a Somali recipe for Ramadan or weddings and other parties. A seasoned ground beef mixture is wrapped in a cone-shaped patty and fried like an egg roll.

Ingredients

- 1 (14 ounce) package spring roll wrappers
- 2 tablespoons olive oil
- 2 pounds ground beef
- 1 leek, chopped
- 2 teaspoons ground cumin
- 2 teaspoons ground cardamom
- 1 teaspoon salt
- 1 teaspoon pepper
- 1 small onion, finely chopped
- 1 clove garlic, minced
- 1 tablespoon all-purpose flour
- 1 tablespoon water, or as needed
- 1 quart oil for frying

Prep Time: 25 minutes

Cook Time: 45 minutes

Ready In: 70 minutes

Makes: 24

Directions

1. Heat olive oil in a large skillet over medium heat. Add onions, leek, and garlic, and cook, stirring until the onions are transparent. Add ground beef, and cook until about halfway done. Season with cumin, cardamom, salt, and pepper. Mix well, and continue cooking until beef has browned.

2. In a small dish or cup, mix together the flour and water to make a thin paste. Using one wrapper at a time, fold into the shape of a cone. Fill the cone with the meat mixture, close the top, and seal with the paste. Repeat until wraps or filling are used up.

3 Heat the oil to 365 degrees F. (170 degrees C.) in a deep fryer or deep heavy pot. There should be enough oil to submerge the wraps. Fry the sambousa a few at a time until golden brown. Remove carefully to drain on paper towels.

Research

- Find out why people were at war in Somalia when Liban was a child. You can start at *http://news.bbc.co.uk/go/em/fr//1/hi/world/africa/country_profiles/1072611.stm*.

- What language(s) do Somalians speak and why? Why might Liban's parents have good English skills? Look at *http://countrystudies.us/somalia/51.htm*.

Activities

Some activities related to Liban's story:

Schools (in the section Cultures and Customs)

Holidays and Celebrations (in the section Cultures and Customs)

Buddies and Sponsors (in the section Linking the Classroom to the Community)

People Weren't Allowed to Have Businesses

Name: Romina

Age: 18

Home country: Uzbekistan

Residence in U.S.: Pennsylvania

Romina is my name. It isn't Russian, it's Italian. Russians listen to lots of different kinds of music from many different countries. My father loves to listen to the Italian singer Romina Power. I'm named after her. My last name is from Uzbekistan—that's where we're from. We're Sephardic Jews, and we're Bukharian. We all speak Russian.

We came to the U.S. in 1991 when I was five years old. We had lived in the capital of Uzbekistan, Tashkent. Most of my family was already moving to America, and Uzbekistan was still communist. People weren't allowed to have businesses—but my dad always had his own businesses. They wanted to take him to jail—one guy saved him and bought the businesses before the KGB found him. We were chosen to come to the U.S. on a visa; most people had to come through Italy to come here, but we came straight here.

My father has since traveled back to Uzbekistan three times, and my mom has gone twice. I haven't gone back yet, but I'd like to go there on vacation someday and see what it's like—it's my homeland.

I don't remember too much since I was so young, but I remember that it was a lot different in Uzbekistan—kids had more free time, we played outside, and picked apples and fruits from trees. We were encouraged to go into sports or dancing—all of these lessons were free, but it was a lot stricter there. My brother took gymnastics—when he first started he was afraid to jump, and they'd beat him until he got it right.

It was acceptable to get involved in dance or sports—there was nothing to do if you didn't go into those. I remember having a TV, but there were no video games. We would just play outside with rocks and stuff.

I remember playing with my brother, making animal faces and ice cream cones out of mud. And there was this guy who came by with a wagon with toys and gum. Gum was really hard to get—that's my strongest memory—always wanting to get gum! Our family would give the man bottles to recycle, and in return he gave toys or gum. I was also always stealing gum from my aunt.

Our most important food is *pilaf*—rice, carrots, and meat. If guests came over, you'd always make that and/or *shish kebab*. These are our most traditional foods—even today, when we have guests over that's usually what we serve them. We also ate these foods on the May 1st celebration—to celebrate the first day of spring—that's a big holiday in Uzbekistan.

Uzbekistan is a Moslem country. The Russian Moslems didn't like Jewish people, so we couldn't say we were Jewish. There were lots of Jewish people where we lived, but we didn't tell people if we were around groups of Moslems. We were allowed to come to the U.S. because we were Jewish.

When we came to America it was different; none of us spoke English and it was very hard for us. I was only 5, but one of my brothers was 13, and another was 11. We always had TESOL [Teacher of English to Speakers of Other Languages] classes; it was easier for me to learn the language because I was a kid. But my brother, who is now 26, has an accent, and so do my parents.

When we first came here, my brothers were made fun of because of the way they dressed. People would pick on them because they didn't have money for nice clothes and called them "dorks."

I remember going to school in the U.S. at six or seven—I would cry every day when I first came and always wanted to go back home. I had none of my friends here, and I didn't understand the language. People also treated me differently because I dressed and acted different and I didn't speak English. Most of my friends were Russian. It was good that there were a lot of family members and Russian people living in my city. I was lucky to have a Russian student teacher in kindergarten. It helped a lot to be able to speak Russian with her. In about one-and-a-half years, I spoke fluent English.

It's sad that some people lose their Russian language—it's great that I was able to keep speaking Russian. Some people my age have bad Russian or didn't learn how to speak it from their parents. I might take Russian in college. There might have been a cultural club at my high school—I'm not sure. People pretty much stayed within their own cultures and cliques.

My best friend is Yelena. We became friends five years ago. I met her at my cousin's birthday party— her older brother was going out with my cousin. We've been best friends ever since. We don't go to the same school, but we know the same people. In our county in Pennsylvania, all of the Russian people know each other. Yelena's family is from Ukraine, but we all speak Russian.

I guess a defining moment in the U.S. for me was when people started counting me as an American and not Russian. Whenever I'd say I'm Russian, people would say, "You're an American."

Now we live in a suburb of the city we lived in for six or seven years. I've just graduated from high school, and I've already started as a freshman in college, majoring in pharmacy.

Becoming a pharmacist in Uzbekistan would be a lot harder. The schools there are not as great, and it would be really expensive. It is also hard to get good money for a job. Here it is different—we can get loans, financial aid, and stuff like that.

I really want to become a singer—that's my biggest dream. I even had a manager, but not the greatest one in the world. I have a CD out but it is mostly dance music. My parents know that I love singing. In Russian restaurants—they're more like clubs—people have a chance to get up and sing. Whenever we go, I always sing a song. My parents would like it if I became a singer, but they want me to get my degree first.

My mom didn't have a chance to go to college, so she really wants us all to be educated. Both of my brothers finished college, and I am starting college. My mother doesn't want me to have to rely on a husband—she wants me to rely on myself.

All of my family has businesses. They didn't have a chance to go to school, so they all opened businesses. My dad's always taken chances on businesses—he isn't scared to lose money; he lives in the moment. My dad wants me to go to college, but he doesn't believe in me as much as my mom—he thinks I'll spend all my time going out. But when I graduate from college, he'll be the proudest one of all.

I'd advise newcomers in the U.S. to learn how to communicate with American people; learn the language. Most people feel like an outcast at first. Have a plan of what you'll do, how you'll get started and all that. Also, make new friends. It will be hard in school but get through all that—it was hard for me, but it taught me a big lesson.

Make sure you have American friends too, and they'll help you out. Don't only be friends with Russians—have a variety of friends. That's the biggest mistake of some people in my community—they're only being friends with Russian people. Sometimes they're here for years and don't know the English language well or have bad accents.

Americans don't know a lot about other people's cultures—they only eat American foods and listen to American music. They don't expand their horizons like Russians do. Russians eat different cultures' foods and listen to different kinds of music. Americans should try more new things so they can appreciate differences more. Teachers and parents need to learn about different cultures, foods, and music. I remember that my teachers didn't seem to understand that I needed time to learn the language.

Americans should try more new things so they can appreciate differences more.

Students should know that just because someone's different doesn't mean that they're a dork or that they're stupid. They should open their horizons to other people and not just stay in their own cliques—they should go out of their way to meet other people. Even me, I didn't do that enough, and I have mostly Russian friends—that's not the way to do it.

It was hard to adjust, but I lived through it and I am happy to be in the U.S. and not where I came from. I am happy that I lived there, and I'll go there on vacation—but it would still be very hard for me if I lived there.

Questions

1. Find Uzbekistan on a map. Look at the surrounding countries, especially the ones to the north and south. What do you know about those countries?

2. What is the KGB? What is the closest equivalent to the KGB in the United States?

3. Romina's family traded with a man who could get them toys and gum. Why didn't they just go to the store and buy what they wanted?

4. Why does Romina say her family was "allowed to come to the U.S." due to their religion. Do you know any places in the U.S. or the rest of the world where people say they don't like each other because they are of different religions? Why is that?

5. Do you agree with Romina that it is easier for young children to learn another language than for older people? Do you know kids from other countries who have no accents? Do you know older people who do?

6. Why do you think Romina thinks it's sad that some people from Russia lose their ability to speak Russian? Have a discussion at school or in a club meeting about the advantages of knowing more than one language. Decide what foreign languages you think would be the most useful for Americans to know and why.

7. What do you think of Romina's dream to be a singer and her parents' wish for her to get a college education first? What do you hope to do? Do your parents agree with your plans? Why or why not?

8. Why do Romina and other young people stay in cliques with friends who have backgrounds sim-

ilar to their own? If you do that too, think about why and what you might do differently to expand your group of friends.

Research

* Research the history of the U.S.S.R. in the twentieth century. Find out why people in so many countries spoke Russian, like Romina's family in Uzbekistan and her friend Yelena's family in Ukraine.

* What does the word *Sephardic* (Sefarad) come from? Do you know anyone who is Jewish? Are they Sephardic? Where did their ancestors come from? What language(s) do/did they speak? Here's a website about Bukharan Jews in Uzbekistan: *http://www.jewishvirtuallibrary.org/jsource/ History/islamtoc.html*

* Look up the definitions of "immigrate," "emigrate," and "migrate." What is the difference? How do the definitions relate to stories in this book?

Activities

Some activities related to Romina's story:

Meaning of Names (in the section Cultures and Customs)

Why Do People Want to/Have to Leave Home? (in the section Immigration and Citizenship)

Who Lives Where? (in the section Immigration and Citizenship)

Language Help (in the section Linking the Classroom to the Community)

I Was Born in a Refugee Camp

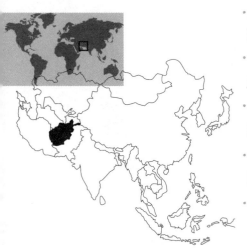

Name: Inayet

Age: 21

Home country: Afghanistan

Residence in U.S.: Colorado

People call me Inayet now but my full name is Inayetullah, which means "gift of god" in Arabic. Our names are picked by our elders. I am an Afghani Muslim. Afghanistan was conquered by Muslims in the seventh century. I speak the Afghan language of Pashto but I can't read or write it. My parents are from Afghanistan but they had to go across the border into Pakistan because of the Soviet invasion of my country. I was born in a refugee camp close to the city of Peshawar, Pakistan.

My dad came in to the U.S. in the early 1980s. I'm not sure why he came to the U.S., but Afghanistan was occupied by the Soviets and the camp in Pakistan wasn't a place to start a home. He worked odd jobs and lived in the back of someone's home. The homeowner became a friend and they are still friends today. In 1991, after he established himself in the U.S., he came back for the family.

I went to school in the refugee camp in Pakistan. We were physically abused more often than we were taught something. If you couldn't spell *cat,* they would slap your hand or body with a tree branch. I still have a long scar from being hit by a teacher. The schools were set up by the Pakistani government. There was nowhere else for the refugees to go. The educational system was only to make an appearance, not really to educate. There was no means of ensuring sanitary surroundings and there didn't seem to be any hope. In Afghanistan there was the war. In Pakistan, the Afghan refugees were treated with contempt. From my perspective growing up, it seemed that the Pakistani government wasn't favorable to us.

I was about eight or nine when I left Pakistan. I remember coming to the U.S.. I was put in a tutoring program. The tutor was so nice. I would expect a blow or slap or punch whenever I made a mistake, but she never did that.

In Pakistan, I was too young to differentiate between norms and values. I realized when I came to the U.S., though, that because my mom only had a third grade education, education was the most important thing. My mom would bang on my door and yell "Wake up, wake up!" every morning.

My parents were always encouraging me to do better and telling me it was important even though they couldn't help me with my homework. Now I'm in college. I don't know what the end result will be, but I know that if it wasn't for my parents continually reminding me and encouraging me, I wouldn't have made it this far. Education was at the forefront.

Both of my parents are very religious. They are deeply faithful. In communist Afghanistan, there was resistance to the occupation because they were trying to keep people from worshipping God. When they came here to the U.S., they could worship freely without worrying that someone would come to the door and kill them or take them to prison. My mom almost always prays five times a day. My parents' faith has an effect on me, too.

My mom used to cry a lot when we first came to the U.S. Back there, there were always people to talk to. Here she was always alone. She didn't know the language or have any friends. She got used to solitude over the years, but that was the most difficult aspect for my mom.

Elementary and middle school were very rough years. I didn't understand English well. Kids would mess with me. Punch me. They'd tell me to curse at teachers, and I would do it without understanding. Then the school would call my dad, so I'd be punished at school and at home. I got suspended a lot during those years because students would trick me into getting in trouble, and I didn't know how to defend myself in English.

I remember in elementary school, this girl that I met said, "Go back where you came from." People don't understand that you would have to go back to a war zone or a refugee camp. Those comments are emotionally painful. I was young and didn't know how to explain that my country was full of bombings and murders, and occupation by the Soviets. We were the lucky ones to come to the U.S., and we expected Americans to know why we came, but they didn't know.

Then nine or ten years later I saw the same girl again, and she apologized.

In high school, I worked on my English, and I understood what was happening around me. The same students who got me into trouble also became more mature. I was more accepted in high school. I said hello to everyone in the hallways, but stuck to myself. At first, I was a friend to everybody, but a friend to nobody.

I always looked at other kids and wished I could hang out with them. Eventually, I worked up the nerve to ask kids if I could hang out with them after school. But I thought it was *so boring*. As soon as that happened, I realized that I didn't have to worry about hanging out with the "cool kids" or a particular group. I wouldn't hang out with a group; I would go home and study because my parents were so focused on academics. In high school, I served on the environmental committee.

I met my best friend in high school French class. He sat behind me and we somehow became friends. His name is Phillip. We still keep in contact with each other. Phillip is white. He's a big guy. I don't know why we became friends. He'd have dinner with my family. At his house, we'd put food in the microwave and play video games and hang out. Phillip is starting community college now, and thinking about going to medical school. He drinks a lot of alcohol now, which is something I don't do.

Now I'm a student at a state college where I also volunteer at the radio station. I work with a nonprofit organization that helps individuals with special needs do recreational activities (rafting, museums, dances, shows, etc.). I also volunteer at the Afghanistan Student Association on campus; we bring speakers to raise awareness at our college and do projects to help Afghanistan. The association is open to all students. I want to work with others and come up with positive solutions. People participate in groups to have end results together.

I don't even know what the average American knows about Afghani culture. People think that we're all terrorists. They ask me, "Are you a terrorist?" People say that to my face—mostly joking. I think, "How do you want me to respond?" It's a very stupid question. Afghanis are not terrorists. Yes, there is oppression in Afghanistan because people are poor. They are fighting over there because it was used as a testing zone for all the latest weapons.

Comments that I hear now about terrorism are painful. *Terrorist* is a very derogatory term for Afghanis, and it's ignorant to ask a person if they are a terrorist. It puts you in a very awkward situation when you are asked such a question. The reason I don't answer is because I don't want to give them power over me. If you don't answer it gives them something to think about. I don't want to answer a question like that because they don't deserve an answer. Americans don't understand the history and that we faced terror ourselves. I can't understand why they seem to think it's funny to ask if we are terrorists.

People talk about how oppressed women are in Afghanistan, but why do people only talk about that as part of the Taliban? Females are still being oppressed now that the Taliban is gone. People only respond to what they hear on television. Now that the Taliban is gone, people have stopped worrying about Afghani women.

> If you don't know the history, you can't understand the culture, the music, the politics, and the situation of Afghani refugees in the U.S.

The most important thing for Americans to learn about Afghanistan is the history from 1973 when the king was overthrown through 2001 and up to the present. If you don't know the history, you can't understand the culture, the music, the politics, and the situation of Afghani refugees in the U.S.

My dreams for the future would be to work with the U.S. government or with nonprofits in Afghanistan, because I believe that what the U.S. did in Japan and Europe post-World War II was important. I believe the U.S. should help Afghanistan recover: education, human rights, and economy. I just want to do my part. God gave me the opportunity to come to the U.S. to study. How can I use this knowledge to repay the country of my parents? What if I was left in Afghanistan? Would I want someone who had my opportunity to come back and help? Yes. I have an obligation as a U.S. citizen to help them, or I've wasted my opportunity.

My advice to new immigrants is that learning the language is the most important thing for newcomers in the U.S. Second would be to focus on education and to have the goal to go to college. In the U.S., education is valued, so those who want to help themselves and help the world can do that through education.

The only thing I would suggest to teachers is that they should just be compassionate and know where immigrant students came from. Know their struggle. Don't make it easier for them because of pity, but have compassion. Want them to be the best, and don't make excuses for them academically because in the long term that can be harmful. Know that it will take them a long time to communicate in English, so also have patience.

My advice to American students is to not take advantage of immigrant students' lack of language skills. Help them out. There were other students who would help me read and learn the language; it was just the few who were hard on me and who made life very tough. So, help newcomers learn the language and culture.

The U.S. provides opportunities for people to come here and make their own lives the way they want. My dad made a life for us here. He never had a higher education. He became a taxi driver so that he could provide for me, and so I could do better and advance. In Pakistan, I would probably just have to become what my father was in life. I don't know for sure why my dad chose the U.S., but I think it's because whatever religion you follow, you don't have to worry that someone will come and take you away to prison. There is not that fear here; in the U.S. we have freedom of religion and economic opportunities. Freedom to live.

Questions

1. Have you ever made a bad joke or said something to a fellow student that you wish you hadn't said? How did the person react? What would you do differently if you could take back what you said?

2. Inayet experienced peer pressure in several ways: Pressure to do things others told him to do without understanding the effects; pressure to try and become a part of a group that he didn't have anything in common with or didn't enjoy. Have you had similar experiences? If so, what did you do? How have you found friends you can enjoy and trust?

3. Have you ever had an experience where you didn't know how to behave—maybe attending a concert, visiting someone else's religious services, or eating in a restaurant that serves foods you don't know? How did you react to being so clueless? Did you trust someone to tell you what to do? Did anyone ever trick you? How did that make you feel?

4. Inayet talks about feeling lonely, and how lonely his mother felt without anyone who shared her language and experiences. Do you think being alone is the same as being lonely? If not, what is the difference? Have you ever been lonely? What did you do?

5. Inayet feels strongly about working in groups because it lets other people get to know him and he learns about other people's ideas. He likes participating in groups to come up with positive solutions. What are your experiences in working in groups? How are your experiences with groups the same as and different from Inayet's?

6. What are the similarities and differences between Inayet's story and the stories of Roya, Romina, and Tim?

Research

- Inayet admires what the U.S. did in Japan and Europe after World War II. Do you know what he is referring to? If not, do some research to find out.

- Research the history of Afghanistan and match the facts to the circumstances Inayet describes in his own life. How was Inayet's life affected by his country's history?

  (See The Columbia Electronic Encyclopedia at *www.infoplease.com/ce6/world/A0856490.html* and Afghanistan interactive maps at *www.nation algeographic.com/landincrisis/drought.html*)

Activities

Some activities related to Inayet's story:

Your Family's Immigrant/Migration Story (in the section Immigration and Citizenship)

Religion (in the section Cultures and Customs)

What We Learn from the Media (in the section Stereotypes, Tolerance, and Diversity)

What Are Stereotypes and Why Do We Use Them? (in the section Stereotypes, Tolerance, and Diversity)

I Am Told I Have No Nationality

Name: Anne Rose

Age: 19

Home country: Haiti/French Guyana

Residence in U.S.: Connecticut

I was born 19 years ago in French Guyana, which is north of Brazil in South America. It is a territory of France and the culture is basically French. My parents were both born in Haiti. There was much poverty and turmoil so they left Haiti in search of better educational and economic opportunities. They moved to French Guyana where I was born, but had to leave there also because it was so difficult for them to establish citizenship and their status was not secure.

My parents wanted to come to America in search of a better and safer life for themselves and me and my sisters. When I was about two years old, my mother came to the United States. I went to live in France, where my father and uncle had moved in search of work. They worked long hours and it was difficult for them to care for a little girl, so I went back to French Guyana to live with friends of my family. This couple became—and I still consider them—my second parents. My father soon joined my mother in the U.S., but then it took seven years for my paperwork to be approved to come here.

During those seven years, the couple I lived with in northern French Guyana was pretty strict, so I did not have a lot of freedom or time to roam around unsupervised. But I had friends who I played with—we played sports, games, walked around the city, and sometimes slept over at each other's houses. Since people in French Guyana were not always accepting of people from other backgrounds, I never told my friends I was of Haitian descent.

I don't think many people know very much about French Guyana—some people confuse it with Ghana, which is in Africa—so they don't even know it is in South America and that it is a French territory. I think people would be surprised to learn that the standard of living there is quite high and that, like in France, university education and other services are very inexpensive.

French Guyana resembles France in customs and culture. It was relatively easy for me to adjust to the U.S. because of the similarities between a basically European-influenced country and America. I am still missing French Guyana and the couple who raised me. I hope to visit the country again soon and certainly look forward to seeing both of them and the whole family soon. I miss the country and them very much.

Bastille Day is a national holiday in French Guyana, like it is in France. But the most fun holidays were the week-long festivals—like Carnival—that each city in the country held in spring and summer. The festivals were really fun—there were games, rides, concerts, and fireworks, and parades where people wore outrageous costumes. Carnival is also very big in Brazil and during our celebrations, many Brazilian people often came and celebrated with us, bringing their own special music and costumes.

In 1997, at the age of 12, after many trips to different embassies and tons of paperwork, I came to the

United States. I went straight to the airport after getting clearance. I hadn't even told my friends I was leaving and didn't get to say good-bye to them. One reason they didn't know anything was because I kept it hidden from everyone that my parents were Haitian and that I was living with friends. French Guyana is a beautiful place, but people who were not French were often looked down upon.

I was only 12 years old and didn't speak English—just French—so the plane ride by myself was pretty scary. No one understood me and I didn't understand anyone else or what was going on around me. But when the plane landed, my father was there to greet me and he took me to our family's home in Connecticut.

> No one understood me and I didn't understand anyone else or what was going on around me.

My parents as well as my "second parents" in French Guyana were and still are very committed to seeing that all their children get a good education. In French Guyana, I went to public school until the sixth grade.

When I first came to the United States and was to go into seventh grade, my mother insisted that I attend a parochial school because she heard that the public school kids were very mean to kids who were different and who didn't speak English. I spent two months in that school and I cried every day. There were no ESL classes and the teachers didn't understand French. I didn't understand anything they were saying or what was written in my books. And I was expected to just do the work anyway without any help. Also, at home my parents spoke Haitian Creole, which I didn't understand, and my sisters didn't speak French. So it was difficult both at home and at school to communicate.

I learned Creole as well as English, and then things got better for me pretty quickly, especially after two months when my mother allowed me to transfer to the public school.

Not only were there ESL classes to help me learn English quicker, but it turned out that everyone was really nice. I was the "French girl" and the kids all were friendly and curious about me and my background. I made friends quickly and also ended up in the top of my class by the end of eighth grade.

Today I still live in Connecticut with my family and work at an international institute. The institute helps new refugees and immigrants with housing, English classes, and various immigration and adjustment issues. I also am a sophomore in college, majoring in sociology.

After finishing college, I plan to be a social worker or guidance counselor so I can help children either in high school or in college make good choices in school and life so they will have a better chance of achieving their goals. I think I would have had the same opportunities to complete my education and realize my career goals in French Guyana as well, and for a lot less money!

I am very involved in my church, which encourages community service. I am the secretary of my youth group and I and other church members help newly arrived Haitian kids and young people with their adjustment to life in America. We make a point of letting them in on what the different customs and rules are here and ways they can "fit in" and have a good life here.

My best friend is Chantelle. I met her at my church, which is the Seventh-Day Adventist Church, when we were 14 years old. She is Haitian, like my parents, and we are very close. She moved to New York last year and that was a hard time, a lonely time for me. She is moving back to the area soon, so I am happy about that. On the other hand, she soon will begin college in Alabama, so I will lose her again. It's hard not to have a best friend to do things with and I hope that changes for me soon.

The other frustrating thing in my life now is trying to obtain my American citizenship. Although I was born in French Guyana, it turns out that I am not a citizen of the country because my parents were born in Haiti. I found out that I am not a Haitian citizen either, even though my parents were born there, because I was born in French Guyana. It is a Catch-22—I am told I have no nationality. Now I must wait and wait to obtain citizenship in the U.S.

Young people and children have a lot to learn when they come to the U.S. I suggest that even before they come, if it's possible, that they study about America so they do not feel so much that they are in a strange place. Then, I would say: *get involved in everything you can.* The more things they get into, the more opportunities they will have to learn, understand, and appreciate life here. I always say, "Seek and you shall find." And here that means that if you seek help, you will find good and kind people to assist you and make all the hard adjustments that much easier.

For those born in America, it's so important to try not to make immigrant kids feel different. By reading books about various countries and cultures, Americans would learn and understand more about different customs, values, and ways of interacting and communicating. But these studies should be part of the regular school curriculum, not just a study lesson when someone from another country arrives. It's also critical to be friendly and really go out of your way to make newcomers feel welcome and to help them if you see that they are having difficulties.

Questions

1. What does it mean to be a *territory* of another country as in French Guyana? What is Bastille Day and why would it be celebrated in French Guyana?

2. Why do you think Anne Rose feels so attached to her "second parents" in French Guyana? What adults other than your parents do you feel close to and why?

3. Rent the movie *The Terminal.* Compare and contrast the situation of Tom Hanks' character with that of Anne Rose's dilemma. How do you think each one feels and why? How would you feel in their situation? What would you do about it?

4. Anne Rose refers to her situation as a *Catch-22.* What does Catch-22 mean? What is the origin of the phrase?

5. Have you ever been reluctant to tell people something about your background? Why? What would have made you more comfortable in sharing your background with them?

6. What do you think of Anne Rose's recommendation that cross-cultural studies be part of the school curriculum in the U.S.? What are you learning in school about other cultures? How could you learn more?

Research

*   How is the history of Haiti different from that of French Guyana? What similarities are there between the two?

*   Research the rights of "stateless" immigrants such as Anne Rose. What will she have to do to become

a U.S. citizen? The website *www.unhcr.org* and the activity "Why Do People Want to/Have to Leave Their Native Land?" in the section Immigration and Citizenship will help you.

• Do some research on the Seventh-Day Adventist Church. Make a report to your class on the origins and major beliefs of that faith.

Activities

Some activities related to Anne Rose's story:

Friendship (in the section Cultures and Customs)

Religion (in the section Cultures and Customs)

How Does It Feel to Be Different? (in the section Stereotypes, Tolerance, and Diversity)

Buddies and Sponsors (in the section Linking the Classroom to the Community)

I Won't Go Back Unless There Is Peace

Name: Sanuse

Age: 13

Home country: Sierra Leone

Residence in U.S.: Illinois

My name is Sanuse. It means "the sun." I was named after my cousin. I am from Sierra Leone in West Africa. I speak Fula, Krio, English, and French.

We came to the United States because we lost everything we had in our country. There were people looking for my father to kill him. He was shot by someone with a machine gun but he survived. My mother was captured by rebels and we never saw her again. The U.S. accepted us. I won't go back unless there is peace. If there is peace, then I would like to go visit.

The thing I remember the most about my country was when my family and I were still living together. At that time they hadn't captured my mother. My favorite holiday in Sierra Leone was Ramadan. It is the biggest holiday in my country. At that time my friends and I would go to visit friends and family to wish them a happy holiday.

The most important values I grew up with are being honest, working hard, and going to school.

> The most important values I grew up with are being honest, working hard, and going to school.

My family thinks that education is the most important thing in life.

I came to the U.S. in 2003. Now I live in Illinois with my father, stepmother, two brothers, and two sisters. I am in the seventh grade. My best friend in the U.S. is Adrian. We became friends because we were in the same grade and both of us were taking ESL classes.

The situations I experience in school are simple. The students help me with my work. They always ask me about my culture and that makes me feel accepted.

I like to study and to participate in interfaith refugee youth program activities after school. I also like to play soccer and capoeira, a kind of martial art that started in Africa and is practiced in Brazil. I listen to rap music and watch TV comedies like *Moesha* and *Becker.*

I dream to be in the army. If I had realized that dream in my country, I would get killed quickly because many people don't like my family or my father.

I want Americans to know that my African culture is not disgusting like other people think. It's just like any other culture. We have good things and bad things.

I suggest to new immigrants that they try to stay out of trouble and to parents I suggest to watch their kids closely.

I suggest that Americans pay more attention to newcomers. They should try to know what newcomers like or dislike and respect their culture.

Questions

 How did reading Sanuse's story of what happened to his family in Sierra Leone make you feel? Write a few sentences about how you felt and why.

2. Look at a map of Africa and locate Sierra Leone. Why do you think Sanuse speaks so many languages?

3. How do Sanuse's values compare to the values your family holds?

4. In what ways is Sanuse's life like yours? In what ways is it different? Why?

5. Why do you think Sanuse feels that some people think his African culture is "disgusting?" How would you advise him to help change the opinions of those people? (Hint: Doing the first research project in the next section will help you.)

6. Do you agree with Sanuse that all cultures have both good things and bad things? List your opinions of some good things and some bad things about your culture. Share your list with some friends and see if they agree or disagree. How do you decide what is good and what is bad?

7. Do you play any sports, or know of any sports played in the United States that did not originate here? If so, where did they originate? How did they come to the U.S.?

8. If you have never done it before, get to know a newcomer in your school or community. Learn about their culture, and what they like and dislike.

Research

- Research the conflict in Sierra Leone. Who are the "rebels" that Sanuse mentions?

- Look up some Krio proverbs at *www.sierra-leone.org/proverbs.html.* Try to read the proverbs

and see how much you understand; then look at
the English translation below each one. What can
you learn about cultures through their proverbs?
Try to find out more about the Krio language,
where it is spoken and why.

• How did capoeira get from Africa to Brazil? How
do you play capoeira? See *http://www.capoeira.
com.*

Activities

Some activities related to Sanuse's story:

Why Do People Want to/Have to Leave Their Native
Land? (in the section Immigration and Citizenship)

Interview Someone (in the section Cultures and
Customs)

Living in a Global World (in the section Linking the
Classroom to the Community)

The Hmong Have Never Had a Country

Name: Pang Houa

Age: 21

Home country: None—Hmong

Residence in U.S.: Minnesota

My name is Pang (pronounced *pong*) Houa. Pang is a very common Hmong name; it means "flower." My middle name, Houa, means "cloud." Our last names are clan names, so many Hmong have the same last names.

The Hmong people are an ethnic minority everywhere they live. They have never had a country of their own. The biggest concentration was in southern China centuries ago. At the height of their civilization the Hmong had a kingdom. There is no written history of my people. They migrated into Laos, Thailand, and northern Vietnam. They have not been welcome in any of those places and generally have lived as a separate group and as subsistence farmers.

My mother's family lived in northern Laos. Her father was a provincial leader. The Hmong assisted the CIA during the Vietnam War when Chinese troops were passing through northern Laos into Vietnam. So when the U.S. left Vietnam they were in great danger. Being in a high profile position, my mother's family fled south to Thailand, traveling at night and hiding during the day. My father was the only one of his family who migrated. My mother and father met in a refugee camp in northern Thailand. They married when my mother was 16 and my father 18. I was born in that refugee camp.

We lived in two refugee camps. The second one was a processing camp where we were oriented to the U.S. In the first, we lived in long houses that were sectioned off for each family to have a little space of their own. We used outhouses where the toilets were made of stone. I remember not being allowed to sit on the toilet and having to carry some water in a bucket to flush it.

The camp was fenced and Thai vendors would come to the outside of the fence. I remember walking to the fence and buying a favorite food, papaya salad, through the fence. I would hand my coin through the fence, and the woman would reach back through the fence and tie the change in my dress so I wouldn't lose it. And then she would give me my little container of salad. Papaya salad is made with green papaya, which is white and crispy, sort of the like cabbage. It is chopped very finely, and then seasoned with fish oil and very hot peppers. It also has peanuts in it.

The Hmong are mostly subsistence farmers and so large families are important to help with the work. There is also a very high child death rate because of the lack of health care. My family of seven kids is common. Boys are important; the parents eventually live with their son. We usually live in multigenerational households, and my mother has always missed the fact that we did not have our grandparents with us in the U.S. I was sorry, too, to not have grandparents. We used to send cassette tapes to them, but it was not like living with them. I had never seen them until we went to visit them in Laos in 2000. They are subsistence farmers and live in a thatched house. One of my grandfather's favorite grandchildren is in a picture I brought home. The little boy always followed my grandfather around. I learned that the little boy died of some illness. They have no access to government programs and so there is no health care.

There is great respect for elders. The Hmong are ancestor worshippers and believe in shamanism. Shamans are healers, and they are called upon for health problems. I can't remember when we had a shaman, but we do participate in soul calling. Soul calling ceremonies are held at special times of life, such as births, and periodically. The idea is that souls can wander, so they need to be called back. When we do these ceremonies, white strings are tied around our wrists, to tie the soul there. The strings are left on until they fall off. I went off to college with lots of white strings tied on my wrist!

Our traditional costumes are very intricate with lots of embroidery. It was customary to raise the silk worms for the silk and sheep for the wool, spin the threads, dye them with natural dyes made from roots and other plants, and sew them all by hand. It would take months to complete the fancy skirts the women wear. My mother has a real talent for sewing. In the refugee camp, she would make clothes for people, including doing the very intricate embroidery. When I was in high school, she started her own business. She creates lovely clothes without using patterns.

There have been several large migrations of the Hmong to the U.S.: in the late 1970s after the Vietnam War, later in the 1980s to 1990, and now. Approximately 15,000 Hmong are migrating from Thailand to the U.S. now. The largest concentration is around the Twin Cities (Minneapolis and St. Paul), Minnesota; in fact, that is the largest concentration of the Hmong anywhere in the world.

Many agencies that sponsor the Hmong immigrants are faith-based groups. My family was sponsored by a Catholic organization in Wisconsin, where we first lived when we immigrated in 1984. I was four years old.

We moved to Minnesota when I was still young. We lived in a housing project and I went to school with predominantly Hmong kids. We spoke Hmong together and played Hmong games. I really liked to read and was good in school—I guess you would say I was "nerdy." I got status from being taken out of ESL class and put into regular classes faster than some of my classmates.

When I was in fourth grade we moved into a single family house and my parents put me into a private Catholic school. They were concerned about the fact that some young Hmong people were forming gangs. My school was a small parish school—only about 200 students—and nearly all the students were white. I was happy, did well in school, and generally didn't realize there were cultural issues. Many of my classmates' families would go north for hunting and fishing, and once in a while I would hear racist comments like "Hmong are so 'stupid' they don't know they need a fishing license." But generally, as a kid, I didn't notice any discrimination in school.

My parents are sad that they did not have a chance to get an education. Education is very important and they have worked hard to be able to put us in private schools. During the summers they were able to have a garden plot. They would raise as many crops as possible to sell to get extra money for our education. I had to remember why they were doing that when I was stuck at home babysitting during the summer when I wanted to do other things.

Even though I was Catholic, I did not attend the parish church where my school was. Instead we attended a large Catholic church where services were held in Hmong. My parents didn't allow me to play with classmates outside of school, so I never went to anyone's home or anything. Instead, I went home and studied, helped my mom with chores, and then as my sisters and brothers were born, babysat. I have five sisters, the oldest being 7 years younger than I am, and one brother who is 16 years younger than I am.

When I was in high school, I was on the volley-ball team. That was when I first had a chance to participate with the white kids' activities out of school. My brother and sisters have been allowed to integrate much more with their classmates out of school.

When I finished high school, I left home to attend Brown University. I was really excited to be away from home and to get away from things "Hmong." What a surprise I had when there were only three Hmong students at Brown and everyone was curious about my culture; I spent lots of time talking about my background and culture!

I had an opportunity to study abroad in my junior year of college and went to Paris. More surprises. I tried to fit into the population, trying not dress like an American, but I was always identified as an American! (And it was not a very popular time to be in France as an American, because the Iraq war had just started and the French were very much against it.) The other surprise is that I never felt so American as when I was in Paris. I began to understand that I talk and act like an American!

> I never felt so American as when I was in Paris.

I majored in American civilization at Brown. In that major you can select different kinds of classes. I focused on immigration and ethnicity. An internship allowed me to work with the Hmong Development Corporation. It lobbies for legislation that will help immigrants and against things that will hurt or limit them. It also provides educational programs for Hmong parents on many topics. Since graduating last June, I am working for the same group. I am doing policy advocacy and education. It is challenging my upbringing about elders being all knowing; I am young and am frequently teaching and making presentations to people older than I am.

I think I want to pursue a law degree and work either in the area of human rights or something international.

My sisters and brother have had different experiences than I did, as they spent more time with their white classmates outside of school. All of us girls did well in school because, I think, we knew the Hmong language well before we started learning English. My little brother, however, has struggled in school. His teacher made the assumption that he was "slow" without getting to know his family and his situation to try to assess what the real problem was. It was determined eventually that he has language confusion because he doesn't know either language that well. So, I would hope teachers would get as much information as possible about individual children in order to help them in the ways they need it.

Questions

1. What is a *clan?* Do you know anyone who is not your relative but has the same last name as you do? How do you think that happened?

2. What does it mean to be an *ethnic minority?* Who are ethnic minorities in the United States?

3. How would you know the history of your country if it were not written down? Try to tell your classmates about your family history without using any notes. (See the following activity section to prepare your story.)

4. Look up definitions for any terms Pang uses which are unfamiliar to you, such as *subsistence farmer* or *thatched house.* How do those defini-

tions compare to what is familiar to you about farmers and types of houses where you live?

5. If you can find a green papaya, try to make a papaya salad the way Pang describes it and share it with your family. Can you explain the taste to your friends?

6. What is a *multigenerational house?* Do you live in one? Why or why not?

7. What is "ancestor worship"? Describe any spiritual traditions or special clothing that are part of your culture. Why are they important to you?

8. In your opinion, did anyone ever make a mistaken judgment about your abilities? What happened and what did you or your parents do about it?

9. What do the terms *lobbying, policy advocacy,* and *human rights* mean? What do people study and do with a major in the field of human rights?

Research

• Using some of the following books or websites suggested by Pang Houa, learn more about the Hmong and share what you learn with your family, classmates, or club members.

> *Bamboo Among the Oaks* by Mai Nengn Moua. Minnesota: Minnesota Historical Society Press, 2001. A book of plays and stories by first- and second-generation Hmong.

> *The Spirit Catches You and You Fall Down* by Anne Fadiman. New York: Farrar, Straus and Giroux, 1997. This book explores the clash between a small county hospital in California and a refugee family from Laos over the care of a Hmong child diagnosed with severe epilepsy.

www.hmongcenter.org. St. Paul, Minnesota—
The Hmong Center which houses a collection
of dissertations and papers on Hmong.

www.hmongabc.com. A Hmong art, book, and
craft store.

* Do some research on the Vietnam War to find out
  how Pang's people assisted the CIA and why they
  were in danger after the United States left
  Vietnam. How and why did they go to live in
  Minnesota? What is the Hmong Veteran's
  Naturalization Act of 2000? Why was it passed?

Activities

Some activities related to Pang Houa's story:

Meaning of Names (in the section Cultures and
Customs)

Your Family's Immigration/Migration Story (in the
section Immigration and Citizenship)

Religion (in the section Cultures and Customs)

Why Do People Want to/Have to Leave Their Native
Land? (in the section Immigration and
Citizenship)

With Guns Pointing at Us, We Walked

Name: Tim

Age: mid-20s

Home country: Kosovo

Residence in U.S.: Connecticut

My first name is Fitim, which is Albanian for "Victor." In the U.S., and since I was a boy in Kosovo, everyone has called me Tim or Timmy. In my country this is very common—most people are given nicknames. I am planning on formally changing my first name to Tim soon. One reason is because Americans seem to have so much trouble pronouncing Fitim, which should be said *fee-teem*. But I always get called *Fateem,* which is an Arabic name and, besides that, it is a girl's name!

I am from Kosovo, a region of Serbia in the Balkans. I was born in 1979 and lived with my parents, three sisters, and two brothers in a town of about 30,000 people about 25 kilometers [15 miles] from the capital city of Pristina. My family had to leave Kosovo when the Serbian government forced Kosovar Albanians to leave their homes and the country. I was 19 years old.

Like most people in Kosovo, my family is Muslim and of Albanian nationality. Serbia was one of six provinces that were part of the Federation of

Yugoslavia. The region in Serbia called Kosovo was granted autonomy by the Yugoslavian government in 1974, which meant that we weren't completely independent from Yugoslavia, but we were given the right to speak Albanian in our schools and elect local government officials.

Everything changed in 1989, when the president of Serbia, Slobodan Milosevic, decided that Kosovo should belong to the Serbian people and that the Albanian people who had lived there all their lives should leave the country. The Serbian government took away all of our freedoms, including the right to speak Albanian in schools and to hold jobs. My father was a miner in Kosovo, but like all Kosovar-Albanian workers, he was fired from his job and replaced by Serbian workers. Most of the Albanian-speaking high schools in Kosovo were closed then as well. I was only little when all this started, but I was very afraid.

Starting in 1989, there was terrible violence and discrimination against Albanians in Kosovo. People were beaten, shot to death, forced from their homes, fired from their jobs, and not able to continue their schooling. From about the age of 10 on, I lived with fear and insecurity. Even though my town was left alone by the soldiers until 1998 and I continued to go to school while we tried to live our normal lives, everyone in town knew that the rest of the country and the Albanian people were under attack. I worried all the time about what would happen to me and my family.

In 1998, when I was about 17 years old and just finishing my first year of law studies at university—which was actually housed in a private home by this time—our life in Kosovo changed forever. Nearby towns and villages were bombed and all Albanians were forced to leave their homes. Whoever refused to go was shot. Children and their families from surrounding villages then streamed

into our town and soon it was filled with families
with no place to live, no food, no supplies—they
came with just the clothes they were wearing. We
had very little ourselves, but whatever we had, we
shared with them. It was difficult, though, to care
for so many more people.

In March 1999, relatives came to our house with
news. We all sat around a radio and learned that the
United States and Europe had sent bomber planes
to stop the attacks against the Albanians and their
villages. We were overjoyed. Everyone ran into the
streets and started cheering. First there was
absolute silence as we saw the planes, then their
signal lights, and then the explosions as the bombs
dropped. At that moment, we knew our country
was going to be saved. The bombings continued
from March until June 1999. At last someone in the
world cared and was going to save our country. To
this day I would say that the people of Kosovo
regard President Bill Clinton as "our father" or "our
country's father." In fact, one of the main streets in
the capital city of Pristina is now called *President
Clinton Boulevard.*

After the bombings began, the army went on an
even more savage rampage against Albanian people
in Kosovo. This time, our town was not spared. It
was bombed and then soldiers came. They went
from house to house and at gunpoint ordered
everyone to leave. They shot anyone who refused.
With the soldiers pointing guns at us, my family
walked out of our house and into the street. There
already were about 3,000 people walking down the
road. No one knew where we were going to go.
When I looked back, I could see that our house was
already on fire. I now know that it does not even
exist anymore—it burned to the ground.

Without warning or reason, the soldiers started
shooting and people were falling all around us.
Along the journey, one of my relatives was shot and

killed. My father buried him in a field. We walked and walked and were very cold and hungry. After a few days, we found an abandoned house that had flour and sugar in it. We made some bread and some slept while others watched out for soldiers. But then the soldiers found us and again we had to leave and continue our journey. We walked along the highway for several days. Then buses arrived and we were told to board them. Some buses took people to the border of Macedonia, but the bus my family was on first drove to Pristina. There I saw that the police station and the army camp had been destroyed—flattened—by the [NATO] bombs.

Then we boarded another bus and were taken to the Macedonian border. There must have been more than 20,000 people there, all trying to cross into Macedonia, which then was not very agreeable to having tens of thousands of refugees come into their country. When we arrived, many people had been camped there for days without any shelter or food. It was miserable—very cold and rainy. My family and others started walking along the railroad lines trying to find another way into Macedonia. Thankfully, a soldier took me aside and told me where there were landmines planted and to be careful. At last we crossed into Macedonia, and a United Nations' bus took us to a refugee camp near the capital city of Skopje. We joined more than 15,000 people in the camp, where the cold and rain made for miserable living conditions. My family stayed there for one month. During this time, I helped the United Nations workers by translating for other refugees. After about a month, my family received word that we could go to the United States.

We first lived at Fort Dix in New Jersey. The U.S. soldiers were very kind and very helpful. There were lots of activities to occupy the refugees' time,

> I helped the United Nations workers by translating for other refugees.

but I spent my time with the soldiers because I wanted to improve my English and learn everything I could about life in America and what I would have to do to succeed in this new country after I left Fort Dix. There are two soldiers I met there whom I consider my friends today. We still keep in touch through letters and I hope to see them again soon.

After spending three months at Fort Dix, we learned that an international organization in Connecticut was sponsoring our family to help us find a home and a path to a new life. We moved to a city in Connecticut that is about an hour from New York City, and within a few days we moved into a house in the city. My mother, father, three sisters, one brother, and I all lived there. Within a week, I found a job in a bakery. The job started at 3:00 A.M. and was about 20 minutes away from home. I bought a bicycle for $12.00 and rode to work every morning in the dark. It was not an easy job and it was pretty scary riding the streets at that hour, but I needed to help support my family.

After about six months, I was offered a job by the organization that sponsored my family. I love my job and am happy for the chance to help new refugees settle in the U.S. Now, several years later, I am working full-time as a case manager supervisor. I help people find housing, deal with immigration issues, apply for financial assistance, and get counseling or English lessons if they need them. I have a few American friends from work and some Albanian and Lithuanian friends as well. I also am studying at night at a nearby community college. My major is criminal justice. I hope to complete my studies and get a job in the criminal justice field, either as a police officer or FBI agent.

My wife is Lithuanian and has a very close family. We have a beautiful 13-month-old baby girl. We bought a condominium and we live two streets away from my family. They bought a home and my parents, three sisters, and one brother live there. I visit them often and particularly when my mother is cooking my favorite dinner!

Before the conflict in Kosovo, there were many good times. The people in my town and those in other areas of Kosovo had lived there for centuries and everyone knew each other. I remember that in the evenings, the streets were full of people. Everyone came into town and would walk up and down the streets, stopping at cafes, talking to each other, sometimes eating in restaurants. Every night, from 6:00 to 7:00 P.M., cars weren't allowed on the streets. It was very lively with everyone out walking and being with each other. Family and community were very important. We say that days should be spent like this: eight hours working, eight hours sleeping, and eight hours with family.

The best holiday for me in Kosovo was New Year's. Unlike here, it was really more a time to spend with your family than to attend big parties. Everyone went into town and there was great food, music, fireworks, activities, and tables set up for games like cards and dominoes. Everyone stopped to wish each other "best wishes for the new year." We also observed Muslim holidays, such as Ramadan, during which we fasted. But the best holiday is at the end of Ramadan, which we call *Happy Eating Holiday.*

I love American music, but I also often listen to traditional Albanian songs as well. Many songs are about our country and the sadness the war brought. When I listen to these songs, sometimes I cry, so I don't put these tapes on too much. There also is very upbeat and lively gypsy music that I like. My family still cooks and eats traditional Albanian meals. I am not a very good cook, so I visit my parents a few streets away when I want a really good meal. Some traditional meals include *goulash,* which is a stew with meat, potatoes, and other vegetables served with noodles. One of my favorites is a dish called *peeta,* which is made with very thin dough that has a filling of spinach and spices around the edges. Then we fold the dough many times and cut it into squares and bake it.

In Kosovo, family time is very important and life was at a much slower pace. I was surprised when I came here to see how fast people walk. And how loudly they talk. In Kosovo, when people talked loudly it usually meant they were angry and were probably going to fight. This is a small thing, but in Kosovo, shaking your head means yes and nodding your head means no. In America, it is just the opposite. Also, we always greet people, in stores and everywhere, with *hello* and *good-bye.* Not greeting shop owners and others that way is considered rude.

Education is very valued by my family. All the children in my family went to school. When we came to Connecticut, my sister was going to be in her senior year at high school. She was very afraid to go and I had to bring her to the school to make sure she went. Because her English was not very good, the school wanted to put her several grades back, but I convinced them to give her a chance in the senior class. She graduated as an honor student and is now attending a community college.

I sometimes miss my home, and when I do, I visit a neighborhood in the Bronx, New York, that has a large Albanian community. There the streets are alive with people and Albanian stores and restaurants. Albanian Muslims are not anything like the radical Muslims you hear about in the news. We do not wear headscarves and the women are not veiled or banned from education. Our religion is important, but it is not as restrictive and we do not view people of other religions as enemies.

There were many hardships and challenges when I came to the U.S. Like all refugees and immigrants, it is hard to make friends, learn English, understand all the customs and rules, and find steady work to support yourself and your family. I dealt with all of this by working really hard and not dwelling on the negative. I came here at age 19 and had much to learn and to do, so I did not worry so much about making friends as I might have done if I were still in primary or high school. I was too determined to succeed and make a good life for myself and my family. My main disappointment, and one I can't do anything about, of course, is that I wasn't born in the United States.

My advice to new immigrants is to learn and speak English, go to school and study hard, and learn and obey the rules and customs of this country. Take advantage of all opportunities to improve your situation, such as attending ESL classes, youth programs, and programs that improve your skills, so you can find a good job and make a good life.

Questions

1. What is *NATO?* Why did the United States and Europe try to rescue the Kosovar Albanians?

2. What happened to Slobodan Milosevic?

3. What is a "refugee camp?" What are landmines and what do they do to people? What can you do about these situations? (See *http://www.ajaproject.org/sandiegoproject.html* and *http://www.handicap-international.org.UK/)*

4. Tim describes the evenings in his home town when streets are closed to traffic and people walk around, talking with each other, visiting

cafes and eating. Does this happen in your town, perhaps on special days? If not, have you ever visited a place where this happened? Did you enjoy it?

5. Are family and community as important to you as they are to Tim? Why or why not?

6. Why did Tim come to the U.S.? If there had been no war in his country, where do you think he and his family would be living today? How would his life be the same or different?

7. What impact do you think Tim's life experience might have had on his choice of job, wife, friends, free time, music, food, studies, and political opinions?

8. What role did the U.S. soldiers play in Tim's life? How is this the same or different from what you thought soldiers did?

9. Imagine that you are Tim's American daughter. What would you think of your dad's life? How much do you know about your own parents' lives?

Research

• Research the twentieth-century history of Yugoslavia, including the period that Tim describes. Look at maps of the area from different periods to see the ways in which the region has been divided over the years. Find out what the U.S. government did for the Kosovar Albanians at this website: *www.clintonpresidentialcenter.org /legacy/040299-fact-sheet-on-relief-for-kosovar-albanians.htm.*

• The majority of Kosovar Albanians are Muslims but not Arabs. How did the Muslim religion come to this part of Central Europe? See *http://lamar. colostate.edu/~grjan/kosovohistory.html.*

- Tim says he wants to change his name so his nickname becomes is official name. Find out how someone can do that in the U.S. Do you think his parents and other relatives will like the idea? Why or why not?

Activities

Some activities related to Tim's story:

Your Family's Immigration/Migration Story (in the section Immigration and Citizenship)

Holidays and Celebrations (in the section Cultures and Customs)

Values and Behaviors (in the section Cultures and Customs

Why Do People Want to/Have to Leave Their Native Land? (in the section Immigration and Citizenship)

I Didn't Ride a Camel to School

Name: Roya

Age: 30s

Home country: Iran

Residence in U.S.: Maryland

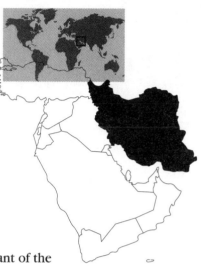

My family name means "descendant of the Imam." Imams (or Emams) are the direct descendants of Mohammad the Prophet. They were entrusted with carrying on the Islamic legacy. Today, those who lead the Friday (Sabbath) prayers, something that only men can do, are called *Emam-Jumaa,* or "Friday Imam."

My last name reflects the influence of spirituality, spiritual leaders, and Moslem theocracy over Persian culture. It also reflects the legacy of being repeatedly invaded over centuries by the Moslems and others, assimilating the new culture and customs, and prevailing as a nation.

I moved to the U.S. to continue receiving a Western education, something my parents prized. Today, I realize that at my private school in Iran I received an education that presented enough information about European cultural history to enable us to think more globally than do most Iranian public school students. Public school students received very strong technical training in mathematics and

science, but they only heard one (Iranian) point of view when it came to history, literature, and social studies.

My parents ended up in the U.S. in the early 1980s, after the fall of the Iranian Shah. They came seeking a country with civil liberties and better economic opportunities. After the Iranian revolution, such opportunities were very difficult to find there. My dad was a doctor in Iran and he had to go through all the American licensing procedures at a very late age in order to practice medicine in the U.S.

In Iran, my favorite holiday was select Fridays (weekends) when my father was not working. He would take the four of us out to a restaurant for lunch and we'd eat *chelo-kabab* (rice and kebabs), something normally eaten only on special occasions because it was very rich and expensive. I felt a happy togetherness that made weekends better than the other days.

My other favorite day was *Now-Rooz* ("new day"), the Persian New Year. It's the first day of spring on the solar calendar, which is shared only by a few countries, as far as I know. I would receive new clothes, help with spring cleaning, and eat Persian sweets that were deep fried by our nanny. She came from a long line of confectioners and her last name was *Ghanadian*, or "of the confectioners." Dad also passed out money, new small bills *(rials)* as gifts.

My parents wanted me to be either a concert pianist or medical doctor. They insisted on sending us to the best schools and getting help for us if we weren't doing well in school. My father believes that education is the only pathway to better living. I also believe this.

The biggest taboo I can think of in my culture is that of the female human body. Islamic countries insist on hiding the female body because of modesty, respect, and tradition. I still look at women who exercise in tight leggings and tops in the U.S. and think how shameful and shocking they would seem on the streets of Tehran. My own sense of modesty is somewhere between the two extremes. During the times of the Shah, it was acceptable to exercise in baggy shorts and perhaps a sweatshirt, but not tight bicycle pants and small tank tops!

My dream was to become a doctor. I had always intended to obey my parents and come to the U.S. for college upon graduation from high school. Our country had a very difficult state university admission exam where 200,000 applicants competed for only 200 places. I was not taught technical subjects in the Persian language, so it would have been nearly impossible to attend an Iranian state college. My school closed after the revolution in 1979 and it was moved to Malaga, Spain. My parents chose to come to America with my brother and me rather than send me away to Spain with my classmates.

Just as in Iran, in the U.S. I had to work very hard to achieve success in school—but not for academic reasons. I was culturally overwhelmed by all of the "advanced" social issues confronting American students, such as sexual freedom, drug use, and all the competition.

> I was culturally overwhelmed by all of the "advanced" social issues confronting American students.

I really didn't have issues with "fitting in" on the outside. I didn't have a noticeable accent and didn't look or dress much differently than most American kids. On the inside, however, I never felt like I fit in *anywhere* until I made little safe spaces for myself over a long period of time. Since foreign (and even some American) students often can't find sensitive people or places at school, I think it's important for schools to have some sort of "sensitivity training" for teachers and students.

I always tried to find my own ways to fit in since I came to the U.S. I have been rejected for different reasons, the worst one being from ignorance about who I am by teachers and classmates. I now realize there are all kinds of people and you should look for the most understanding ones whenever possible. Once I was brave enough to complain to the head of my school. One of my teachers was spreading stereotypes about Moslems and how they shouldn't come to the U.S. because they cause trouble and don't fit in. The principal seemed surprised and said he'd talk with the teacher. I felt good being able to speak up for myself.

I would like Americans to know that Iran is very different from Iraq and Saudi Arabia, that it is not Arabian. Every culture has a subtle difference from surrounding countries that is important to know. For example, the Japanese are very different from Indonesians, but they are both from "somewhere in Asia." I would like Americans to know that most Moslems are very kind and spiritual. They are simply threatened that the strong foundation of Islamic cultural life is eroding as people demand more personal, political, and economic freedom. It's scary to most Moslems who are in charge of maintaining order in Moslem society according to the Koran (our bible.)

I also would like Americans to know that I didn't have an oil well in my backyard and I didn't ride a camel to school, even though I saw a lot of camel caravans passing through the outskirts of my home town, and camels are *very* cool!

In my professional life, I am now working on public policy, something nearly impossible to do in a country such as Iran. I feel that although fear of foreigners is very high in the U.S. right now, and the current economic problems here are lessening opportunities for many, it is my job as a U.S. citizen to constantly push for reforms to improve things so that we may *all* enjoy the American dream.

My most important advice to new residents in the U.S. is to talk to people who can support you. Find people who moved here from your country before you did who are able to guide you. Find students and school counselors of any origin who give personalized attention and understanding.

My advice to teachers is: If you have foreign students, before you meet them, read the *Encyclopedia Britannica* entry for their country. Reading the encyclopedia will arm you with a number of essential facts that could help the students feel as if you know a little bit about the history and culture of their country. Don't tell the students you read it— most foreign students were raised to look up to their teachers and at least at first they feel more secure if their teachers seem to know a lot about everything.

To parents: Visit with foreign parents to see your comfort level at letting your children interact with their children.

To American students: Ask new immigrant students a lot of questions before you make statements and assumptions about them and where they are from. Read the encyclopedia or a good book about that student's country and ask them questions about what you have read. Do tell the students you read it because they will feel good that you cared enough to take an interest in them and their culture.

Questions

1. What is a theocracy? What is a "shah"?

2. Where does your name come from? What meaning does it have for you and your family? How is the origin and meaning of your name similar or different to Roya's?

3. What do you feel is your best subject in school and why?

4. What cultural history have you been taught in addition to American history?

5. What is your favorite holiday and why? How do the reasons for liking the holiday compare to Roya's?

6. What is your dream for when you grow up? Who or what has influenced your dream? Why?

7. What do you think of Roya's advice to teachers, parents, and students? Why? Read about Iran or another country from which one of your classmates comes and try to follow Roya's advice. Describe what happens.

8. What are more ways in which you can help new Americans feel welcome?

Research

• Learn about the Iranian solar calendar at *www.iranmania.com/Information/Iran_Inform ation/Calendar.asp*.

• Learn more about Islam and the role of women in Islam by looking up the lessons on *www.ran-domhouse.com/highschool/catalog/display.pper l?isbn=0-8129-6618-X&view=tg*.

• Read about the fall of the Shah of Iran and the 1979 hostage crisis.

• Find a recipe for kabobs. In what countries are they popular? Try making a recipe that sounds good to you.

Activities

Some activities related to Roya's story:

Religion (in the section Cultures and Customs)

Family Rules (in the section Cultures and Customs)

Holidays and Celebrations (in the section Cultures and Customs)

Values and Behaviors (in the section Cultures and Customs)

My Culture Did Not Value Individualism

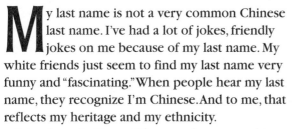

Name: Jina

Age: mid-20s

Home country: China

Residence in U.S.: California

My last name is not a very common Chinese last name. I've had a lot of jokes, friendly jokes on me because of my last name. My white friends just seem to find my last name very funny and "fascinating." When people hear my last name, they recognize I'm Chinese. And to me, that reflects my heritage and my ethnicity.

I was born in Guang Zhou, and we moved to Hong Kong when I was little. I remember when I was younger in my native country, Chinese New Year was such a big holiday for me. I'd get so excited during that time of the year. I loved all the Chinese New Year food and the tradition. Ever since I moved to the States, I definitely miss it.

One thing I remember vividly is that when I was growing up, I felt like I had to be like everyone else or else I wouldn't be accepted. It seems in my country, you are taught not to be an outcast. I think the culture back there didn't promote individuality at all. That's why when I moved here, I was thrilled to see how many different kinds of people are here, truly a melting pot.

The most common value that I grew up with is that girls are supposed to grow up to be housewives and know how to do domestic chores very well. Even when they're in the workforce, they're supposed to be doing secretarial jobs. Just to sum up, girls' roles are to support men. My mom has been a career woman all of her life. She always strived to be different and prove that a woman can do an equally good or even a better job than her male peers. She got her master's degree in English literature.

I think to a certain extent, American society also possesses the value that women's roles are to be a support to men. At the same time, women are bolder and more willing to take chances over here, which allows them to explore the world and develop skills to be career women. I love that as compared to the mentality which I was supposed to grow up with in China.

My parents came to the U.S. to pursue a better life. Since both of them have their master's degrees, they definitely expect me to get a master's degree someday in the future. To them, education builds a great foundation for the rest of life. When I was growing up, they'd do anything to push me to do better in school and they were very involved with my path of education.

I was 15 years old when we moved here. High school was very different from what it would have been like in China. In China, the only thing that everyone thinks about is to try their hardest to get into the best college possible. They study 24 hours a day and basically have no social life. There are no junior or senior proms. You've got so much more social life in high school here in the U.S. than in China.

When I was in high school in California, I'd participate in club activities where people of different cultures get to hang out with each other. We'd have activities like international nights, where kids of different cultures cook meals of their own and we'd get to taste different kinds of food.

The defining moment for me in the States was that I was the piano accompanist for our high school choir. When I came to the U.S., I felt like I didn't know how to get to know the American kids and teachers. Music has definitely been the bridge. I remember that one moment when I played a song for the entire choir; the conductor and the choir kids stood up and applauded for me. It was the moment I felt like I was accepted. And ever since then, I became more open to other people and more myself when I meet friends.

Right now, I have friends of all different ethnicities and backgrounds and I feel like I have been accepted by the U.S. society. My best friend is June. She and I were roommates in college. We became friends because we just felt very compatible with each other.

I majored in international business at college. After I graduated, I worked for two years and decided to pursue my dream of working in the music business. So I started going for the music business program through university extension. A vice president of a music publishing company was the speaker for one of my classes. After the panel discussion, I went to talk to her and told her about my interest. A couple of weeks later, I got an e-mail from her informing me that there was an internship opportunity at her company. That's how I obtained my internship in music publishing.

Music is the biggest passion in my life. I started playing piano at the age of five and I also play some guitar. I still believe that music is definitely the way to connect people from different cultures. When we're at a music festival, it doesn't matter what culture you are from; people just feel united by the music and want to find out more about each other.

My dream for the future is to be able to work in the music industry and contribute to what I've loved all my life. I thought about being a musician, but right now, I've come to the conclusion that even being on the business side of the music industry is fulfilling enough for me. I think it would be a lot harder for this dream to be realized in China or Hong Kong than in the U.S. There are a lot more opportunities in the U.S. as compared to my native country, where everything is centrally controlled for the music business. Here, there are a lot more independent record labels and people are more open-minded about the kind of music they're making.

My parents are not very happy with my decision to work in the music industry at all. They have always wanted me to obtain something that they would consider a professional job, such as lawyer, doctor, or accountant. My parents are still trying to persuade me to become a CPA [certified public accountant] instead of trying to get into the music business.

If I encounter a particular challenge or disappointment, I always take it like a chance to prove myself. I've overcome many challenges in my life. I think that people are more resilient than they think they are. So whenever I encounter any kind of disappointment, I tell myself I can get through it and try my best to overcome it.

I am the person I am today because I have always been very open-minded. That's very important for newcomers, so that they don't shut people out when they see things that they are not used to or that they haven't seen in their own countries. If they just keep an open mind, they will discover life in America is full of possibilities and fun.

I would suggest American teachers, parents, and students to keep an open mind as well. I know

> I want everybody to know that we, even of a different ethnicity, possess the same human traits.

there's a certain truth to stereotypes about cultures, but I want everybody to know that we, even of a different ethnicity, possess the same human traits. We're passionate, we're caring, and we get upset just like the other American people do when generalizations are being made.

Americans also should be patient. Newcomers—I know I was—are very sensitive and timid when they first move to the U.S. They don't know whether they will ever be accepted, whether people will discriminate against them because they're from another country and don't speak the language as well as people who grew up here. If people are nice to them, newcomers would feel more willing to learn instead of sticking themselves in a shell and just being with their "own" kind. I think the most important thing is to make them feel that they're just human, like everyone else.

Questions

1. When people hear your last name, do they know your heritage and ethnicity? How do you feel about that? In some cultures, children have the last name of their mother. What difference would that make in people's perception of your ethnicity?

2. Jina seems to think that American culture promotes individuality, at least more than Chinese culture does. Find at least three examples in Jina's story that would make you agree (or disagree) with her opinion.

3. Have a debate in your class over whether a woman's primary role in the United States is to be a support to men. Try taking the opposite side from the one you feel is true!

4. Do you think that music is a bridge between cultures? How so? Give examples and/or bring in music from different cultures to listen to in class to help you decide.

5. How did Jina get her internship in the music business? Pair up with a classmate and role-play that one of you is trying to get an internship in your dream field of work. Switch roles! What did you learn?

6. How do you react when your parents don't approve of something you want to do? Give examples of challenges you have overcome and how you did it.

7. What are stereotypes and why does Jina believe there is "a certain truth" to them? Do you agree or disagree? Why? Is there such a thing as a positive stereotype? How do you feel when someone stereotypes something about you, either in a positive or negative way?

8. Have you ever felt stuck in a shell, just being with your "own" kind? How did you get out of that feeling?

Research

- Research the history of Hong Kong. How did its governance change recently? Why? What is its population, in numbers and ethnicities? What is it most known for?

- Jina is a musician but also has found the business side of the music industry interesting. What jobs are there in the music industry besides being a musician? Do some of them require advanced educational degrees? Which, if any, of the jobs sound interesting to you? Why?

- Research the Chinese New Year: when it happens, how it is celebrated, what special foods are eaten. How is it similar to or different from the way you and your family celebrate New Year? See *www.c-c-c.org/chineseculture/festival/newyear/newyear.html.*

Activities

Some activities related to Jina's story:

How Does It Feel to be Different? (in the section Stereotypes, Tolerance, and Diversity)

Values and Behaviors (in the section Cultures and Customs]

What Are Stereotypes and Why Do We Use Them? (in the section Stereotypes, Tolerance, and Diversity)

Welcoming Activities (in the section Linking the Classroom to the Community)

We Had No Clue about Poverty

Name: Jacque

Age: late-20s

Home country: Mexico

Residence in U.S.: Washington, DC

My name is Jacque. I come from a long line of Mexican family members who speak at least three languages. My father was a diplomat.

I was 10 years old when we moved to the U.S. We lived in the Virginia suburbs of Washington, D.C. In Mexico, my sister and I had attended French schools. They were very strict about everything: clothing, behavior, which colored pen to use in which notebook. My father thought it would be good for us to attend public schools in the U.S.

Even though my older sister and I both spoke English, we were placed in ESL classes. We had many shocks—among the greatest was the way students interacted with teachers. But we also had no clue about poverty and had never been around kids different from ourselves. Now we were in classes with students from all over the world, including a refugee orphan from Vietnam and the daughter of an advisor to the Shah of Iran. We faced a bias by some teachers who thought that ESL students were not serious about school, either that they were "spoiled rotten foreign kids" or that they were not going to stay in the U.S. and school here did not matter.

I had some great ESL teachers. I still stay in contact with some of them. They focused both on language and culture. They encouraged us to join sports and clubs so we could develop relationships with American kids. I was encouraged to join the school choir and a guitar group. We played concerts. I really liked it. Our teachers also encouraged us to join sports teams: soccer, basketball, track. In Mexico girls do not usually do these things.

It really worked. As we got to know American kids, we began to see how our values differed. In Mexico, we learned a lot about culture. We thought a great weekend was going to a museum and a classical music concert with our family. Some of our classmates were shocked by this. We were shocked by students using drugs...we had never heard of drugs in Mexico.

We didn't know American slang. Students were always correcting our strange-sounding English, often teaching us something that was grammatically wrong!

Once I got going in school, I took an accelerated course. I graduated from high school at the age of 15.

I went back to Mexico for college. There I had to take lots of make-up courses in the summer because I had not had several history and other courses that were required in Mexico. At the university, I started a major in English literature but later I changed to human development and sciences.

While living in the U.S., I realized I was gay. I was lucky to have a really good counselor who helped me deal with this. My parents and extended family did not deal with it well at all. It was not such a big deal to be gay in the U.S., but there was little tolerance for gay people when I went back to Mexico.

As part of my university graduation requirements in Mexico, I began working with the poor. With some other young women who had lived in Europe, I started the first women's center in my city. We counseled women about domestic violence, sexually transmitted diseases, self-esteem, and personal development. None of us who were founders of the center realized how much work would have to be done before this type of program would be accepted in the Mexican culture. The government saw us as a threat and planned to prosecute us. I returned to the U.S. to seek asylum.

> **My interest in civil rights became my life's career.**

Living away from my country and culture I came to realize how rich and beautiful Mexican culture is, and how similar we all are as human beings. Being in the U.S. helped me to see how little I knew about my own culture and it made me curious about it. I learned more about Mexico so I could share with my American friends. In the process I became more curious about others peoples' experiences, cultures, and languages. My interest in civil rights became my life's career.

Now I am working in civil rights policy analysis and outreach. I spend time with ESL students and teachers, and do training programs for service providers, such as the police, who do not necessarily know how immigrants perceive them. I coordinate city-wide dialogues on race in a program to help people get past the stereotypes that we all have.

Questions

1. If Jacque and her sister already spoke English, why do you think they were placed in ESL classes when they arrived in the U.S.?

2. Why do you think girls wouldn't play sports in Jacque's generation in Mexico? Did your mother (or grandmother) play any sports in school? Why or why not?

3. How would you define *culture?* Share your definition with your classmates. (Refer to the Introduction for some ideas.)

4. What do you consider to be a "great weekend?" Can you describe a great weekend you have had with your parent(s) or other adults?

5. Have you ever traveled away from your home state or country? If so, how did being away make you feel about home?

6. Do you agree with Jacque that it is "not such a big deal to be gay in the U.S.?" Why or why not?

7. Why would the Mexican government have seen Jacque and the women's center she and her friends founded as a "threat?"

Research

- What does it mean to *seek asylum?* Who is eligible for this status in the United States? Look at this website for some answers: *http://uscis.gov /graphics/services/asylum/.*

- Learn more about Mexico: its Indian and Spanish history, geography, and culture. Does your research help you better understand why Jacque might not know about poverty and people different than her own family? Does it help you understand why her idea of a women's center might not be a popular idea?

- What is the meaning of *civil rights?* What different careers address civil rights? In what ways?

Activities

Some activities related to Jacque's story:

Friendship (in the section Cultures and Customs)

Your Family's Immigration/Migration Story (in the section Immigration and Citizenship)

Values and Behaviors (in the section Cultures and Customs]

Why Do People Want to/Have to Leave Their Native Land? (in the section Immigration and Citizenship)

My Brothers Were My Best Friends

Name: Jeff

Age: mid-20s

Home country: Philippines

Residence in U.S.: Virginia

My name is a combination of Anglo-American and Filipino. Like most contemporary Americans, I don't know the origins of my name apart from the fact that my first name, Jeff, is distinctly Western. My last name is Filipino. We use *Visaya* (a southern Filipino dialect) at home. I am in the middle; the third of six brothers. Only the three older brothers still are able to speak *Tagalog* (a northern dialect).

I was born and lived in rural Philippines until the age of 10. I lived three more years in Fiji. I came to the U.S. at the age of 13. Now I live in Virginia.

It was a simple life in the Philippines. We lived in a small *barrio* [village/town] comprised of farmers and fishermen; simple people with simple needs, governed by a God who was always giving and providing.

Living in an extremely Catholic country like the Philippines has many benefits. It seemed as though every single saint is celebrated in the form of a *fiesta.* My birthday happened to fall on the day of *Our Lady of Mt. Carmel* (July 16). I was revered as a special child to be born on such a day. I was expected to have the heart of a saint. (I did not have one.)

Extreme respect for my elders was a value I held dear. I remember during the first week of school in the U.S., I was in awe as to how students spoke to teachers. There was such a lack of respect for adults and there was no order in the classroom.

My mother is an American. She has a Peace Corps mentality of you either "sink or swim." She refused to place my brothers and me in classes for second language speakers; to her we were regular kids. Those were some of the toughest years of my life. My mother knew how strong we were even if we were not aware of it yet. As our mother's children, nothing could break us. My parents are brave and strong individuals whose values I am proud to emulate.

When I was a boy, my brothers were my best friends. We had moved from place to place so much that we were unable to attach ourselves to friends long enough to label anyone as a best friend. High school was an extremely difficult stage for all of us. I remember how hard it was to eat alone in a cafeteria full of your peers. I pretended to read books as I ate, pretended to be okay, and I was horrible at pretending. Each one of my brothers has a story but we rarely told our parents how hard it was for us. We knew our parents did not have it easy either. We all turned to each other for the "best friends" we lacked.

My oldest brother was a senior in high school when we arrived; he went on to study at the Juilliard School of Music in New York. He has a baby that just turned one. The baby has blonde hair and fair skin and does not look at all Filipino (maybe it's a good thing).

> I remember how hard it was to eat alone in a cafeteria full of your peers.

My second oldest brother played rugby but I don't remember him ever hanging out with teammates on or off the field. He was accepted, I believe, but chose to be with us. He went on to study philosophy in college and later joined the military. He is currently a captain with a command position: he's been deployed in Bosnia, Kosovo, and Iraq, and in January he went to Afghanistan. I am very close to him.

I played rugby as well, following my brother, and I also did a lot of art in high school. There was not really an "art" crowd during high school, but I loved the fact that my paintings and drawings received a lot of attention.

My younger brother was the athletic one. He went on to state championships as a wrestler, shot-put thrower, and one of the best hitters in football. Being an athlete placed him in a position to be popular or accepted. Instead he had the worst time and worst transition. He is a big kid, but a very gentle kid. He is a child at heart and he was the one who was never in fights even when provoked. He opted out of college to join the Marines and fought in Iraq. The fifth brother had a similar path, athletic and joined the military.

Our youngest brother was probably the only one of us who had a good transition; he was in elementary school when we arrived. He does not speak any Filipino dialect, but he does understand.

There was never a defining moment when I could say, "I am an American now." It was a very slow and awkward process of being "Americanized." After the first year I became fluent in English, gained the ability to hide most of my accent, shed the FOB (fresh off the boat) look, and eventually became less of a target for scrutiny. My appearance was one of my biggest paranoias. I received a major beating the first

week of school by two boys in Metallica t-shirts. They did not like "Kmart-wearing Asians." To this day I refuse to shop there for clothes.

As for stereotypes, I'm not sure. I have stereotypes myself. There is a reason why stereotypes exist...there is some truth to them. Yes, I'm a rice eater, but I don't know karate. I don't eat dog, but I sure do love SPAM. I am not good at math, but I sure am great at video games. With respect to my culture...part of my upbringing does not allow me to impose myself on anyone. I am a guest in this country; it is I who have to adapt to what my host provides.

I became a teacher in the U.S. I don't know what my dreams would have been if I had remained in the Philippines. What I do know is what this county has done for me. I am now a sharp contrast to that little child who walked barefoot with water buffalo on the way to school. My brothers and I have grown to love this country, and this is probably why we chose to give back and serve in the classroom or in the military. We are all so proud to be here.

To new young immigrants I say: Remain a strong family and grow as a family. Do not fight change. You will grow to love this country and one day you'll call it home as I do.

To American kids and teachers, I'd say that acceptance begins in the heart. Children are very aware and no superficial "welcoming ceremony" or cultural awareness workshops can influence this part of the individual. I did not want someone to be aware of my cultural differences or needs; I remember just wanting someone to say "wuz-up" or to give me a "high five" or to ask me to a dance...all the little things that would have made me feel "normal."

Questions

1. What does it mean to either "sink or swim?" Write an essay about a time when you had to do one or the other and what happened.

2. What role(s) have family members played in Jeff's life and his adjustment to the United States? Can you describe the roles your family members play in your life?

3. Is there a story about your life that you haven't told to anyone? Imagine that you are Jeff's parents reading this for the first time. How would you feel? What would you say to Jeff?

4. Jeff says he fits some stereotypes about his culture but not others. How about you? Which stereotypes fit you (or one or your friends) and which do not? Why do we use stereotypes?

5. Do you agree with Jeff about just wanting to feel "normal," like other Americans, or would you rather have people show an interest in your native culture and individual needs? Why?

6. Help your school to have a "Mix It Up Day" where students have to sit with people they don't know during lunch in the cafeteria. Discuss with your classmates how this felt. How did your feelings relate to Jeff's stories about eating alone, worrying about his clothes and his accent, and so on?

Research

- Jeff uses two Spanish words, *barrio* and *fiesta,* to describe parts of his life in the Philippines. Find out what language(s) are spoken in the Philippines and why. See *www.gov.ph/about phil/general.asp.*

- Jeff moved from the Philippines to Fiji. Learn more about Fiji and other Pacific Islands by looking at *www.fiji.gov.fj/publish/history_culture.shtml;* Map of Fiji at *www.fiji.gov.fj/publish/fiji_ map.shtml*

- Look up the game of rugby. How is it played? Where did it originate? Where is it played today? Compare and contrast it to soccer and U.S. football. If you have an opportunity, attend a rugby game. Look at *www.geocities.com/koolade /rugby/history.html.*

Activities

Some activities related to Jeff's story:

Friendship (in the section Cultures and Customs)

What Are Stereotypes and Why Do We Use Them? (in the section Stereotypes, Tolerance, and Diversity)

Buddies and Sponsors (in the section Linking the Classroom to the Community)

Part 2

Activities and Resources

Three key concepts—learning, connecting, and belonging—are interdependent and critical to making sense of a new, complex, and even frightening world environment.

Hearing and reading about different values and beliefs may challenge us. If we learn more about ourselves, our roots, and our history, we are better able to understand, interact, and connect with people who have a different history from our own. This is a key step toward building a strong community where all people are valued, included, and given opportunities to belong and contribute.

The activities that follow are a starting place for you to help those in your family, school, and clubs to learn more about yourselves and the newcomers to your school and neighborhood. There also are activities to help you make your immigrant classmates and neighbors feel welcome, get connected, and ultimately become integrated into their new communities in the United States.

The activities are divided into four sections:

1. Cultures and Customs
2. Immigration and Citizenship
3. Stereotypes, Tolerance, and Diversity
4. Linking the Classroom to the Community

The activities are sorted according to the following categories and icons:

 Read About It!

 Research It!

 Write About It!

 Talk About It!

 Think About It!

 Put It All Together!

A chart, starting on p. 241, indicates which audiences can use each of the activities.

Cultures and Customs

Often we don't know much about our own culture, especially if we have lived in one place most of our lives. We're most likely to discover what we like and dislike, and what we call right and wrong, when we encounter someone who behaves or believes differently than we do. That's because we learn our culture's rules, values, and beliefs gradually as we grow up: at home, at school, at our place of worship, and in our friends' homes. And everyone around us behaves very much the same.

As we grow up, we are corrected when we behave in an unacceptable way—wearing the wrong thing, saying something unacceptable, forgetting to thank someone, not arriving at school on time, and so on. We are corrected, but rarely does someone explain why. For example, you have probably heard something like, "You are late to school. For punishment you must stay after school for 15 minutes and write about your inappropriate behavior." But you probably have never heard anyone say, "You know that Americans are expected to arrive on time for school, doctor's appointments, religious events, meetings with friends, and so on because we think time is money. You only have so much, and it isn't good to waste it—yours or others." But the second part tells you about the belief that results in the kind of behavior that is expected of you.

When we travel to a different country or a person moves from another country to our community, we have the great opportunity to learn about ourselves as well as them. As we find people saying and doing things differently, we may think or say they are right or wrong. This is a clue that we have been taught a different value or belief in our own culture. If we take the time to understand what values are in conflict, we will learn about ourselves as well as the newcomer.

In this book you have read stories about young people who have moved to the United States from many different countries. They reflected on things they missed from their countries and what they found different, and sometimes difficult, about living in the U.S. The activities in this section will help you discover some things about yourself and your culture that you may not have ever thought about. The more you know about yourself, the more you'll be able to feel comfortable with and make friends with people who are different. You will be able to talk about your own beliefs and values as you learn about theirs.

Meaning of Names

Perhaps you have never thought about your name other than whether you like it or not. In the *Kids'* stories most of them talked about how they were named and what their names mean.

 Find out the following information about your name and see if you learn something new about your heritage.

1. Do you know why you have the name you do?

2. Does your *first name* have a special meaning? Is it the name of a parent or relative? Did it come from a religious tradition? Is it a name that is currently popular in the United States? If so, what is the basis of its popularity? Or is it unique, perhaps created by putting together several names or other criteria?

3. Do you use a *nickname?* Is it a shortened version of your first name, a name that refers to a physical characteristic, or something you or others just chose? Are there times when your parents use your first name rather than your nickname? If so, when? Why?

4. Do you have a *middle name?* If so, does it have a special meaning or significance to your family? Where you live, do girls keep their middle names when they marry, or do they use their father's or mother's last name as their middle name?

5. Last names (surnames) often give us clues to our cultural origins. Do you know the country of origin of your last name? Talk with your family to learn about it. Sometimes names were changed when people immigrated to the United States: they may have been translated from another language or have been Anglicized (made "more English") so they were easier to pronounce or not look so foreign. Maybe your family name was changed because people from that particular part of the world were being discriminated against at the time your ancestors immigrated to the U.S. Historically in some countries, people took the last name of their town or the name of their

occupation. See what you can learn about the origins and history of the last names of your family members.

Family discussion: Talk with family members about your name. A discussion of family names may lead to interesting discoveries.

In class or clubs: Research your own names. Over the period of a week or several club meetings, have some students put their names on the board and describe their meanings, heritage. (See *Experiential Activities for Intercultural Learning*, Vol.1, page 53.)

· ·

Friendship

Who your friends are depends on a variety of things. If you have lived in the same community all of your life, you probably have longtime friends. If you have relatives nearby, you may think of some relatives as friends as well. If you have moved from place to place, making friends may look different. If you have several siblings and move often, brothers and sisters may be your closest friends. Friends may be of the same age or come from different generations.

Think about your own situation and answer the following questions:

1. What is your definition of friendship? Who are your friends? Do they all live in he same place you currently do?
2. Do you have a best friend? If so, answer the following questions.
   * *Who is he or she?*
   * *When, where, and how did you meet?*

- *How long have you been friends?*
- *How is this friend different from your other friends (what you do together, what you do for each other)?*

3. Have you ever had a different best friend? If so, why is that person no longer your best friend?

4. What do you do with your friends?

5. Do you have any special obligations to your friends (things you would do for them that you don't do for other people you know)?

6. Did you list any of your family members or relatives as friends? Why or why not?

7. Do you call people friends whom you just say "hello" to but never spend time with? If so, why do you think you call them friends?

8. Have you ever moved? If so, how did you make friends in the new place you lived?

9. Do you have any friends who come from a country, culture, religion, or race that is different from yours? How do you deal with those differences?

10. How do you think your answers compare with some of the references to friends in the *Kids'* stories? (You might want to go back to a story or two and find out what the people say about friends.) Why might they be different?

Classroom and clubs: You can individually answer the questions, and then in small groups compare and discuss them. Or, you might answer them as small groups. If there are students from other nationalities, they might be mixed with the other students or form a group of their own. When the groups share the results of your discussions, if differences emerge, this can lead to further discussion.

PTAs and communities: Adults can do this activity as well. It is a good entry into discussing how selection of friends is related to other values, such as strong extended families or more independence among family members, and so on.

Holidays and Celebrations

Holidays are important in all cultures. Sometimes we just celebrate them but don't understand their meaning. Do the following activities to learn more about the holidays your family honors.

Name					
Origin and purpose (religious, historical, other cultural, national, personal)					
Where celebrated?					
Who attends?					
Customs or rituals (foods, clothes, gifts, or other exchanges)					
Duration					

Find or make a twelve-month calendar. Identify all of the holidays and celebrations that your family honors. List some of the information asked about each. If you don't know the answers, discuss the holidays with your family.

1. What is your favorite holiday? Why?

2. If you could invite someone from another country to one or two celebrations with your family, which would you pick? Why? How would the celebration tell them something about your culture? Your values?

Family discussion: Ask each family member to discuss which is their favorite holiday and why. Consider inviting newcomers in your community to one or more of your celebrations.

In class or clubs: Do the calendar activity mentioned in this section. On a large calendar that you can keep, mark all holidays celebrated by students in your class or club. Take time to have each one explained, on or near the date, and participate in some of the activities of the day, if possible (for example, dress, rituals, dances, and foods).

Religion

In many of the stories in this book, the *Kids* talk about the importance of their religion or assistance they have received from religious groups. Learn more about religion in the United States by doing some of these activities.

Surveys of Americans show that a very high percentage of them say they believe in God, believe in an afterlife, and attend religious services regularly in some house of worship. Do some research to find current statistics on these kinds of questions. Here are some websites to get you started: *www.religioustolerance.org/rel_comp.htm* and *www.ncccusa.org.*

Several fundamental values held by many Americans are often traced to religious roots. These include self-improvement, strong work ethic, material success, public education, importance of the individual, anti-authoritarianism, volunteerism, philanthropy and humanitarianism, and self-discipline. Define and then divide up these descriptions of values among your family members, classmates, or club members, and research their ties to religion. Share the findings of your research. If you do find a religious connection, discuss how you think these may have become cultural as well as religious values.

It has been said that no other nation has experienced the development of so many new religious groups or has so many practicing religious denominations. What religious groups were founded in the United States? When? What factors were involved in their founding? A place to start your research is *www.adherents.com/rel_USA.html.*

Roya talks about Iran being a *theocracy.* Raoul says India is a secular country. What do these terms mean? What kind of country is the United States? What does the First Amendment to the U.S. Constitution guarantee to all citizens? What does it mean? What are the current discussions about the separation of church and state related to? After doing some research, discuss some of the current debates on religious issues with your classmates, trying to understand both points of view.

Some seemingly nonreligious institutions in the United States today have historical ties to religions and immigrants. Research the founding of the YMCA (Young Men's Christian Association). How do houses of worship assist newcomers today?

Today, as well as historically, established religious denominations and evangelical groups have played both spiritual and social roles in the United States. Use the following questions for your class or club to explore the broader roles of religious groups in the U.S. today.

1. Make a list of religious groups active in your community. Start with those to which members of your class or club belong to. Find others by using the telephone book.

2. Organize yourselves so you visit a representative sample of these religious institutions. Share with the class or club the weekly bulletin or other written materials that you bring back from your visits.

3. Create a chart to compile data on events that the place of worship provides or supports. Your chart should include religious services and perhaps religious classes for various age groups, plus other activities for adults, young people, and children. It may also include outreach activities—foreign or domestic missions, support for orphanages or other social services, and community activities.

4. Discuss the findings of your research. Ask young people from other countries if they would have similar findings if they did this project in their country. Why or why not?

5. Reread the stories in this book. In what activities of places of worship in the United States have the *Kids* participated?

Adapted with permission from *Living in the U.S.A.,* Youth For Understanding International Exchange, Washington, D.C. 1994.)

Map of Your House

In all cultures there are both public and private places in a home. In some cultures, guests can only be in formal rooms, such as a living room or family room; it would be improper to be in the kitchen (considered a workspace) or a bedroom (considered too personal). On the other hand, in some cultures sitting and talking in a bedroom might be perfectly normal, or guests may stand or sit in the kitchen as the hostess is finishing dinner.

The way rooms in the house are used is both cultural and personal. Do this activity to learn more about how your family thinks about public and private spaces and activities.

 Draw a map of the rooms of your house or apartment. Label each space.

1. Think about who uses each room. For example, everyone may use the kitchen and living room/family room, but only certain people may use each bedroom or certain bathrooms (if there is more than one.)

2. Are any rooms "off limits" to some family members? For example, maybe children can't be in the parents' bedroom or bathroom, or an older brother is not allowed in his younger sister's room. Why do you think there are these rules?

3. If family members are doing the following activities, which rooms would they be using?
    - Watching a movie on TV.
    - Studying and doing homework.
    - Eating breakfast or dinner.
    - Playing with a friend (younger children).
    - Listening to music or talking with a friend (older children). Would the location be different if the friend was of the same sex? Opposite sex?
    - Having a serious conversation with a parent.

- Having friends over for a meal.
- Other?

There are also cultural differences about how it feels to be alone. Some cultures encourage independence and spending some time alone, while in other cultures being alone is not valued or encouraged, and therefore it may not "feel" good to be alone. These values may contribute to how space in the house is used. It's useful to know what your family's customs are and to attempt to make guests feel comfortable when invited into your house.

In family discussion: This is an interesting exercise to do together. It may raise some good conversation about values parents are trying to impart to children.

In classroom or clubs: Do the exercise individually, then share your findings. Try to link some of the rules of the house to values.

Public and Private Behaviors and Topics of Conversations

Just as the use of certain rooms in the house may differ in how they are used (see the previous activity), so do certain topics of conversation and behaviors.

Have a family discussion about what information your family considers private. That is, what topics would you *not* be expected to talk about with friends or acquaintances? Some topics to consider:

- Political preference
- Religion

- Salary
- What things cost (e.g., clothing, cars, sports equipment, and so on)
- Health issues
- Sports teams
- Grades in school

How would you feel if someone asked you a question about something you consider private? Why might people from other countries ask questions you think are too personal?

In some cultures children, girls, and women do not go places alone. Talk about what things your family members can/should do alone and which ones should be with others. Does it matter if the family member is female? Some examples include:

- Children walking a few blocks to school or home from school
- Going to a local store/shopping center
- Getting dressed only in one's own bedroom
- Trying on clothes in a store
- Walking a few blocks to a friend's house
- Going to a public bathroom or swimming pool
- Going to the movies with a mixed group of boys and girls

As you become acquainted with families from other cultures, you may find that they have different customs in terms of public and private topics of conversation and behaviors. It is useful to have discussed your own customs before you learn about those that are different. In order to make friends, it may be helpful to watch for differences. For example, for a new acquaintance from another country to come to your house, your mom or dad may need to go meet that person's family first, and tell the family that their son or daughter is welcome to come to your house.

Family Rules

All families have—and need—rules. Rules are the established guidelines to aid in living together. We usually think of family rules in terms of money, chores, curfews, and so on, but many rules are unspoken expectations of the way we should behave. For example, often there is a long-standing assumption that things are done in a certain way, such as asking permission before bringing a friend home or raiding the refrigerator, or expecting that everyone must clean up his or her own dishes after having a snack or meal. Each family also has more subtle rules, such as children should not express anger to their father. Most family rules are based on values, such as children must respect adults or children must clean their own rooms; some may be the result of family circumstances, such as both parents working, or children having to share bedrooms with other siblings.

A good exercise for the family is to sit down together and list all the rules, spoken and unspoken, that everyone can think of. Everyone should participate and no one should judge the rules. Unspoken rules are more difficult to think of, perhaps, and may be more difficult to talk about as they usually have to do with freedom to comment, emotions, and societal taboo areas. Some may be more difficult to learn and some more "sacred" with more feelings attached if the rule is violated. Some examples of unspoken rules are that children should not criticize their parents; parents never talk about money in front of their children; no one talks about anger or aggression or love; and no matter what happens, everyone is expected to be appreciative.

Family rules can vary in different cultures, even when there are shared values. For example, respect for elders may be valued but shown in different ways. As we interact with people from other cultures in our homes, it is useful to be mindful of our own rules, be prepared to witness other behaviors, and perhaps be ready to explain some of your rules to children or parents of different origins.

Adapted with permission from *Host Family Handbook,*
Youth For Understanding International Exchange,
Washington, D.C., 2005, pages 11-12.

. . . .

Pets

Many families in the United States have one or more pets. Many different kinds of animals live in homes, and some pets are treated almost like people.

If your family has pets, discuss how your family views them. Some things to talk about:

1. What values and beliefs are related to having pets?
2. What educational value do parents see for their children having pets? For example, are children in the family responsible for feeding the pets?
3. What is your reaction to people who don't like pets? Is it the same for those who just don't have pets or are allergic to pets? How do you accommodate friends for whom pets are problematic?

In some cultures, animals have different roles, even dogs and cats. Religious, cultural, and personal beliefs are strong. If people from other cultures are uncomfortable with pets (or certain types of pets) in the house, it may be difficult for them to visit your home.

Foods

Food is important in every culture, and not just for nourishment. Many of the *Kids* in the book cite foods that are essential to particular holidays, others describe their favorites, and several mention eating together with family or others as having particular significance.

If you did the chart for the Holidays and Celebrations activity (earlier in this section), you probably noted some traditional foods for your family or perhaps your religion. In addition to traditional foods, we all have favorites.

What are some of your favorite foods? Pick one and do some research to find out the origins of that food. Where did pancakes originate? Hot dogs? Pizza? Tacos? French fries? How did these foods come to America? When?

Why do you think we call our most familiar foods "American" foods? When you have a chance, ask someone from the country of origin of a food or a dish what they think about the "American" version? How is it different? Is it a popular food in their country?

In class or clubs: Trace the origins of your favorite foods. Use a world map to track how foods have moved. Investigate and write about the different ways foods—or key ingredients—were transferred from one place to another. Create a menu (or a lunch) that reflects foods from all over the world that are commonly eaten in the United States today.

. . . .

Routines and Rituals

The routines of daily life make us feel comfortable and confident. Routines and rituals are cultural; we learn them as we grow up. It may be a shock or lead to misunderstanding when people don't use the same routines. It's easy to criticize or stereotype kids who don't know the routines you have. Many activities can be used to reinforce the multiple ways of doing things, thereby eliminating the need for judgment.

Learn a few phrases in the languages spoken by classmates, and take turns opening and closing the day with phrases such as "Good morning. Today is ____. The weather is ____." "Class is over." "Be safe until tomorrow." "Good-bye." (Learn the appropriate phrases for the country where the language is spoken. Also learn the meaning of those phrases and why they are used.)

Learn about different welcoming and farewell rituals, and use different ones when students join or leave the class.

Discuss how these rituals are different in different cultures and how adapting a new ritual makes you feel. For example, American students might say, "Hi, how are you?" and then not wait for your answer or not expect anything other than "okay" for a response. Or they might say, "Talk to you later," but you never hear from them. Why? Students in many parts of the world shake hands or kiss each other on the cheek(s) when they say hello or good-bye, whereas in the United States this would be unusual.

Values and Behaviors

Sometimes it is hard to understand culture. That's because most of it is not something you can touch or see. One way to try and understand culture is to think of an iceberg. How much of an iceberg is underwater? 90 percent! Look at the figure of the iceberg.

Art **Clothes** Behavior

style of communication   meaning of success
attitude toward education
ideas about discipline   concept of family
attitude toward animals
meaning of friendship
beliefs about good and evil
attitudes about age

The under-water part of the iceberg shows the things we can't see. The above-water part shows things we can see or hear or photograph—our behaviors. The above the water things are representations of what's below.

For example, all of the *Kids* in this book talk about the value of education. Most say it is one of the most important things; in fact, a good education for them is one of the reasons many of their families' immigrated to the United States. Ramon talks about how his father has become more aware of the importance of education since being in the U.S.

They know about the value of education from what their parents *say* and *do:* their parents expect good grades, they have paid to have them in special schools, they have moved to a different country to give their children better educational opportunities.

Another example is how many *Kids* talk about their ways of respecting elders. Many were accustomed to standing when teachers enter the classroom, some mention not using an adult's first name, and Annie talks about having different language forms for addressing adults.

 Think about examples of behaviors you can see (above the water) that reflect values or beliefs you can't see (below the water). Create a large iceberg visual and watch for and write down behaviors you don't understand in other people. When you discover the beliefs or values that relate to those behaviors (probably through research), put them on the iceberg. Refer to the Family Rules activity or the questions about Pets (both are earlier in this section). These are examples of figuring out how values and beliefs are reflected in behaviors.

Schools

All countries that are not at war have some type of schooling or school system for educating their youth. Schools teach values of the culture through academic and nonacademic subjects. Those values are also reflected in school rules, dress codes, curriculum, and types of discipline, among other things. There is a lot you can learn about the United States and its values by learning more about schools based on the observations of the *Kids* in this book. Try some of the following activities.

Jacque talks about coming to the United States from Mexico, where she and her sister were in an elite private French school. Among the things that shocked them when they attended public schools in the U.S. were that there were kids from low-income families as well as kids from all different backgrounds—they had never been around kids whom they considered to be different from themselves. The U.S. has several different types of school systems, but free public education for everyone historically has been very important. In pairs, see if you can take a survey at your school and another type of school in your town. Ask if the "best" schools are those that have children with different skill levels, from families of different incomes, and racial, religious and ethnic backgrounds, or those where children have similar skill levels and come from families with similar backgrounds. Why do you think you got the results you did?

Several *Kids* talk about coming from schools where students were disciplined with corporal punishment. Define *corporal punishment*. Is corporal punishment used in your school? Why or why not? Ask your parents or grandparents if there was corporal punishment when they went to school. Do some research to find out changes in attitudes about corporal punishment in the United States over the years. When you have gathered some information, have a debate with your classmates about whether or not schools should have corporal punishment.

Lots of the *Kids* in this book say that their parents brought them to the United States in order to have them receive a better education. Research some of the many reasons why children from developing countries might not be able to get the same level of education in their native country as they

could in the U.S. Then find out how schools are
funded in the U.S., and how and why the quality of
education might differ from community to community and from public to private to religious schools.
Discuss the pros and cons of each type of schooling.

Many of the *Kids* in this book talk about making
friends through activities they got involved in at
school—music, sports, or other group activities.
Talk to some administrators at your school and
teachers who sponsor or teach special activities to
find out why they think extracurricular activities
are important. Do you agree? Do you participate in
any? Why or why not?

Roya says, "I was culturally overwhelmed by all
of the 'advanced' social issues confronting American
students, such as sexual freedom, drug use, and all
the competition." Hewan states that, "Sex is taboo
and not allowed before marriage at all. Marriage is
never discussed with school-going children." Do you
think that students should simply study while in
school and not be confronted with other social
issues? Do you have any classes where social issues
are addressed? Do a survey of your classmates and
any of your neighbors who attend different schools
to see what they think about addressing social
issues in school. Perhaps you could share your findings through a report.

Do the Religion activity (earlier in this section)
related to church and state paying particular attention to the debate around school prayer.

School is a luxury, a gift, an honor, in many
countries.

1. Go back to Liban's story and read what he
   says about school during wartime. He says
   he attended Islamic school to study the
   Quran (Koran). What is *Islamic school?*
   Who do you think are the teachers? Why
   might a religious school have been allowed

to operate during wartime? What religious groups in the U.S. operate their own schools? Why?

2. Reread Tim's story. What happened to schooling during the Kosovo conflict? Why? Why do you think Tim was studying law in somebody's home?

3. Look at Ramon's story. Read his description of schooling in the town where he grew up in Mexico. Why wouldn't Ramon have finished high school there?

Many countries have national school systems, where schools all over the country are structured the same way and teach the same things. That is not true in the United States. Recall from history that when the early colonies agreed to organize themselves together for security reasons, they were suspicious of a federal government and wanted to retain as much power as possible. Look up the U.S. Constitution and figure out why each state, not the federal government, is responsible for its own schools.

Although we have a free public education system in every state in the United States, and it is mandatory to go to school until you are 16, there is no constitutional right to an education in the U.S. and only 2.7% of our national budget is spent on education. How do you feel about that? Try this activity adapted from *www.education-world. com /a_lesson/00-2/lp2052.shtml.*

1. Review and discuss the important points of the amendments to the Constitution. Discuss the guidelines for adding a new amendment to the Constitution.

2. Imagine that you have been appointed to committees to create a new amendment. Brainstorm ideas for the new amendment.

(If you have difficulty thinking of ideas, start the discussion with a suggestion, for example, an amendment for children.) Write your ideas on the board.

3. Divide into small groups. Each group chooses one of the ideas. Work together to create a proposal for your group's idea and present it to the class. Variation: If you have access to PowerPoint, create your proposals as PowerPoint presentations.

4. After listening to the presentations, write down the one amendment you think should be added to the Constitution. Tally the choices and note the top choice on the blackboard.

Write Your Own Story

Everyone has a story. Have you ever written yours? Try these activities.

Answer the interview questions (at the end of this section). These are the same questions that all of the *Kids* in this book answered. You may want to do some of the previous activities first, as they will help you answer some of the questions.

1. Turn your answers into paragraphs and eliminate the questions.
2. Read it from top to bottom; add any details or other information you would like.
3. Now you have your own story! Share it with others if you'd like.

In class or clubs: Use the interview questions (at the end of this section) to write your family history.

This might be a combined research and writing project. You may need to get information about your name and country of origin from your parents before answering the questions. After answering the questions, make the answers into paragraphs and add any other information. Add a photo also if you'd like, and create a class book or a display.

Interview Someone

Create stories like those in this book.

Using the interview questions at the end of this section, interview one or more young people from countries different from your own. It will be interesting to find out what in their life was (or is) different from yours. While you are talking with them, see if you can find some things you have in common, too, like the same hobbies or favorite foods, movies, or books.

In class or clubs: Interview students in another class who come from countries other than the United States. Create stories, as described in the previous activity, Write Your Own Story, and develop a hallway display. Or combine the stories you collected with the students' own stories to make a book.

For school, PTA, or community: Use the interviews to create an interesting dramatic presentation called Readers' Theater. From the interviews, select the 8 or 10 most interesting/unusual stories. Create one script by writing an introduction (about how the audience is going to meet some incredible people), selecting the interview questions to be used, and including answers from all of the students or a selected number of answers in random order. (All answers don't have to be used for each question.)

You can either play yourself or someone you interviewed. Have a chair for all "actors" on the stage. The narrator goes on stage and reads the introduction. The actors enter one by one, step to the microphone and say who they are, and take a seat. Then, one by one, each of the interview questions is read by the narrator, and the actors stand and read the answers as scripted. You might create a final line to say in unison, such as, "Now I am a student at _____ school in (name of the town) and I am (or becoming) an American." The production can be made more dramatic with sounds between questions: claps, drum beat, bell, or gong.

This same type of dramatic production can be done with adult immigrants in the community. In this case, the narration might include calling out certain years and referring to what was happening locally, before the speakers tell what was happening to them.

Look at the following references about Readers' Theater:

- *http://bms.westport.k12.ct.us/mccormick /rt/whatrt.htm*
- *http://bms.westport.k12.ct.us/mccormick/ rt/rtadapt.htm*

Interview Questions

Name:
Age:
Home country:
Country of origin/ U.S. state:

1. Where does your name come from and how does it reflect your heritage?
2. Where are you from originally and why did you/your family move to the United States?
3. Where do you live in the U.S. and what are you doing now?
4. Briefly describe your life at home as a youngster in your native country. What was one important tradition/holiday/food and what meaning did that have for you?
5. What are the most important community/cultural norms, values, and taboos that you grew up with and how do they compare or contrast with American values?
6. What are your family's expectations/ involvement/attitudes toward education and schooling?
7. Who is your best friend in the U.S. and how did you become friends?
8. What, if any, community or school activities are you doing now that contribute to better understanding among people of different cultures?
9. What was a "defining moment" that you experienced at school in the U.S. that made you feel accepted by your American peers and/or teachers? If you encountered a particular challenge or disappointment, how did you overcome it?
10. What would you like Americans to know about your culture that runs counter to stereotypes you think they have?
11. What are your dreams for the future? How could/couldn't they have been realized in your native country? In the U.S.?
12. What advice/strategies/activities would you suggest to new U.S. residents (parents

and/or children) for successfully integrating into life in this country?

13. What would you suggest that American teachers, parents, and students do to help them better understand newcomers?

Immigration and Citizenship

You, Whoever You Are

You, whoever you are!...

All you continentals of Asia, Africa, Europe,
Australia, indifferent of place!

All you on the numberless islands of the
archipelagoes of the sea!

All you of centuries hence when you listen to
me!

All you each and everywhere whom I specify
not, but include just the same!

Health to you! Good will to you all, from me
and America sent!

Each of us is inevitable,

Each of us is limitless—each of us with his or
her right upon the earth,

Each of us allow'd the eternal purports of the
earth,

Each of us here as divinely as any is here.

— Walt Whitman
From "Salut au Monde" in *Leaves of Grass*

The stories in this book reflect many of the reasons why people continue to leave their native lands and move to the United States. The *Kids* show a cross-section of many of the current immigrant cultures and how they are adjusting to life in the United States.

By doing the activities in this section, you can learn more about the history of U.S. immigration, who has been moving to the U.S. in recent years, and why and how immigrants become American citizens. Then you can explore who lives in your area and research your own family's immigration story!

. . . .

We Are All Immigrants

Immigration is as old as humanity. Some scientists believe that five billion people may have descended from one woman, the ancestor of us all. That would make all of our first ancestors emigrants if they left the continent of Africa and immigrated to other places.

Get a copy of the Discovery Channel video *The Real Eve* (see *http://dsc.discovery.com/convergence/realeve/feature/feature_02.html*). After watching the video, take an anonymous vote on pieces of paper to see how many of your classmates believe that everyone living on earth can trace their DNA back to a single population of Africans. For those who believe it, how does this influence your view of immigrants?

The first record of human migration into the Western Hemisphere dates to the period between 40,000 and 20,000 B.C. Today, one human being out of thirty-five is an international migrant. The number of people who have settled down in a country other than their own is estimated at 175 million worldwide. This represents 3 percent of the world population, and is comparable to the population of Brazil. Nearly all countries are concerned by international migration, whether as sending or receiving countries.

America has been called a *land of immigrants,* but that is only because its history as a nation is short compared to many other countries. In fact, all countries are lands of immigrants; most just arrived earlier than those in the U.S.! If you are from a family that has lived in the United States for several generations, you may not even think about immigration as a part of your story. But it is.

When European settlers arrived on the North American continent at the end of the 15th century, they were looking for land, riches, and religious freedom. They encountered diverse Native American cultures—as many as 900,000 inhabitants with over 300 different languages. Those whose ancestors crossed the Bering land bridge from Asia at least 13,000 years ago, may be considered the first North American immigrants. You can see how they (and plants and animals) migrated on the National Park Service website at *http://www2. nature.nps.gov/geology/parks/bela.*

If you are Native American or interested in American Indian cultures, take a look at the Cradleboard website *(www.cradleboard.org)* or go to the *Seattle Times* newspaper interactive site to "visit" an original Indian village at *http://seattle-times.nwsource.com/news/local/klallam.*

It is estimated that over a million African-born immigrants, such as *Kids* Hewan and Liban from East Africa and Sanuse from West Africa, now live in the United States. The first African immigrants came to the U.S. as explorers—some say as early as 1200 B.C., but certainly by the time the Europeans started coming to the New World. In the 18th and 19th centuries, however, most Africans who came to the U.S. were forced to immigrate, as servants or slaves.

You can find out about early African immigration and slavery in the United States at the following websites: *www.usnationalslaverymuseum.org/ home.asp* and *http://memory.loc.gov/learn/ features/ immig/alt/african2.html.*

Europeans, East and South Asians, Pacific Islanders, Caribbeans, and Latin Americans also have been coming to the United States for generations, primarily in the big immigration waves of the 18th, 19th, and 20th centuries. You'll notice that there are *Kids* in this book who are recent immigrants to the U.S. from all of these regions.

For more about the early immigration of many of these groups, see the Library of Congress website at *http://memory.loc.gov/learn/features/immig/introduction2.html.*

Here are some questions from the Library of Congress website that you can use for more research into questions of U.S. immigration.

1. How did U.S. government policies and programs affect immigration patterns?
2. How did these policies and programs affect immigrants' assimilation into life in the United States?
3. What role did the distribution of resources (natural and manmade) play in the immigration and subsequent migration patterns of immigrants?
4. How did economic conditions impact the immigrants' experience?
5. Did cultural heritage affect an immigrant's place of settlement? How?
6. What impact did immigrant cultural traditions have on the U.S.?

Who Is Coming to the U.S. Now?

Common misperceptions regarding immigration and its effects on American society often result in suspicion, discrimination, and doubt. Do you know the truth?

Take the quiz at the following website to test your immigration IQ: *www.pbs.org/independentlens/newamericans/quiz.html.*

According to the PBS program *In the Mix (www.pbs.org/inthemix/shows/show_teen_immigrants.html):*

- Over 800,000 immigrants legally enter the United States each year as lawful permanent residents, refugees, or people fleeing persecution.
- Immigrants collectively earn $240 billion a year and pay $90 billion a year in taxes— while only receiving $5 billion in welfare.
- The leading source countries of U.S. immigrants are Mexico, Vietnam, the Philippines, and the republics of the former Soviet Union.
- Nearly three-fourths of all new immigrants intend to reside in California, New York, Texas, Florida, New Jersey, or Illinois.

Why Do People Leave Their Native Land?

This book is about young people who have arrived in the United States in the past 15 years or so. Perhaps they already live in your neighborhood but are not yet described in your history books or on multiple websites. Most of the families whose children are featured in this book came of free choice to the U.S. in pursuit of what they hoped would be a better, or at least safer, life.

There probably are as many personal reasons why people migrate as there are people. Nonetheless, there are some reasons that are common to whole

groups, and they have been given names and classifications, mostly for legal purposes.

Economic Immigrants and Refugees

The United Nations High Commission on Refugees
(UNHCR) determines how immigrants and refugees
are classified. The UNHCR *(www.unhcr.org)*
defines migrants [immigrants] in the following
ways:

> *An economic migrant normally leaves a
> country voluntarily to seek a better life.
> Should he or she elect to return home, they
> would continue to receive the protection of
> their government.*
>
> *Refugees flee because of the threat of
> persecution and cannot return safely to
> their homes in the prevailing circumstances.*

By these definitions, most of our *Kids* are from
economic migrant families; the others are refugees
or one generation removed from them. What are
some reasons why economic migrants wouldn't be
able to find a "better life" in their own countries?

To learn more about the different factors that contribute to the desire or need to leave one's country,
check out the United Nations website called
Cyberschoolbus at *www.un.org/cyberschoolbus.*

1. Pick one of the *Kids* who says his or her
    family came to the United States for a
    "better life" or "better education." Then use
    the Cyberschoolbus site to find
    information to compare data on that *Kid's*
    country with the same types of data on
    the U.S. The site can help you develop bar
    graphs that show comparisons between
    countries on population, health, education,

environment, and other indicators of development.

2. Write a paragraph using the data you found to support the reason(s) why you think that *Kid's* family might have immigrated to the U.S.

3. Do exercise 1 again, but now compare the Cyberschoolbus data on the U.S. with that of the Netherlands, where Kim, another of the *Kids*, is from. What is the same or different about the results of your research this time? What conclusions do you draw on immigration from having done this research?

Migrant Workers

As you read their stories, you will see that brother and sister Ramon and Noemy are *Kids* whose family came to the United States and at first got jobs as farmworkers, picking strawberries and lettuce in California.

A *migrant farmworker* is an individual whose principal employment is seasonal agriculture and who travels and lives in temporary housing. Nearly 40 percent of migrant workers are "shuttle migrants," who "shuttle" from a residence in Mexico, for example, to do work in one area of the United States. Seventeen percent are "follow-the-crop migrants" who move with the crops. Most migrant workers are foreign-born.

A *seasonal farmworker* is an individual whose principal employment is agricultural labor but who is a permanent resident of a community and does not move into temporary housing when employed in farmwork. Forty-four percent of farmworkers are seasonal farmworkers, and the majority of these are U.S.-born.

Read the short biography about United Farm Workers' leader Cesar Chavez at *www.ufw.org/cec-*

story.htm. Write a letter to Cesar Chavez that could be sent to his wife, saying what has happened to the farmworker movement since he died, and mention what struggles they are fighting now and what victories they have won.

Find out more about the organization that Ramon wants to work with—Student Action with Farmworkers—whose mission it is to "bring students and farmworkers together to learn about each other's lives, share resources and skills, improve conditions for farmworkers, and build diverse coalitions working for social change." Source: *http://cds.aas.duke.edu/saf/*

Read about the historic Immigrant Workers Freedom Ride that took place in 2003 at: *http://www.afsc.org/ immigrantsrights/news/retracing.htm*

If you are interested in finding social justice groups in your area, check out the interactive map on the Tolerance.org website at *www.tolerance.org /maps/social_justice/index.html*

Refugees

Are persons fleeing war or war-related conditions such as famine and ethnic violence refugees?

> *The 1951 Geneva Convention, the main international instrument of refugee law, does not specifically address the issue of civilians fleeing conflict, though in recent years major refugee movements have resulted from civil wars, and ethnic, tribal, and religious violence.*

> *However, UNHCR considers that persons fleeing such conditions, and whose state is unwilling or unable to protect them, should be considered refugees. (http://www.unhcr.ch/ cgi-bin/texis/vtx/ basics/opendoc.htm?tbl= BASICS&id=420cc0432)*

Kids Sanuse, Inayet, and Tim are considered refugees in the United States by virtue of having fled the violent conditions in their countries. As Sanuse states, "I won't go back unless there is peace." Sometimes refugees are offered special immigration opportunities. Pang Houa's people, the Hmong, are an example.

If you haven't read Pang Houa's story, read it now. Then go to the following website to find out about the Hmong Veterans' Naturalization Act of 2000: *http://uscis.gov/graphics/publicaffairs/comminfo /hmong.htm.* Why was such an act passed?

Political Asylum

When someone comes to the United States seeking political asylum, like other refugees it is because they are unable or unwilling to seek protection in their own country because of a "well-founded fear of persecution on account of race, religion, nationality, membership in a particular social group or political opinion." *(http://www.unhcr.ch/cgi-bin/texis/vtx/basics/opendoc.htm?tbl=BASICS&id =3b0280294#migrants)*

The official difference between a person seeking political asylum and other refugees is that someone applying for asylum can escape to the border or be inside the U.S. and then apply for political asylum in country (the U.S.). The refugee status application is done outside of the applicant's home country but before coming to the U.S. You are allowed to apply for political asylum even if you are illegally in the U.S. You don't qualify for political asylum if you have participated in the persecution of others or if you have already resettled and gotten permanent residency in a country other than your home country or the U.S.

If you haven't yet, read Sanuse's story. Why do you think that some refugees, such as Sanuse's family, are persecuted in their own countries? Have you ever heard of anyone from the United States who has sought political asylum in another country? Why would that be? For one reason, see *www.truthout.org/docs_04/121204H.shtml.*

Do some online research at *http://en.wikipedia. org/wiki/Cuba* or try the lesson at *http://school. discovery.com/lessonplans/programs/us-cuba/* to learn more about the history of Cuban relations with the United States.

One of the most well-publicized political asylum debates in recent U.S. history was about a six-year-old Cuban boy named Elián González. Read about his case at *www.pbs.org/newshour/bb/law/jan-june00/elian_5-11.html.*

Orphans

How can unaccompanied young refugees find their families?

> *An unaccompanied minor is one "who is separated from both parents and for whose care no person can be found who by law or custom has primary responsibility." (http:// www.unhcr.ch/cgi-bin/texis/vtx/basics/ opendoc.htm?tbl=BASICS&id=3b0280294 #children)*

The number of unaccompanied child refugees varies widely. It often comprises from 2 to 5 percent of a refugee population, and in Europe a United Nations High Commission for Refugees (UNHCR) study estimated that 4 percent of asylum seekers were separated children.

Find out what has been done for children who became orphaned because of the 2004 tsunami in the Indian Ocean. How are the different countries that were affected by that tragedy dealing with all the children who were orphaned? See *http://www. unicefusa.org/site/pp.asp?c=duLRI8OOH&b= 277164.*

How many children are orphans because of HIV/AIDS? What can you do to help? Use one of these websites to learn more about AIDS orphans: *www.avert.org/aidsorphans.htm* or *www.unicef.org/media/media_16287.html.*

In the East African country of Rwanda in the mid-1990s, an estimated 67,000 children affected by the civil war there were reunited with their families. Find out more at *www.savethechildren.org.*

The UNHCR works with other agencies, such as the Red Cross, the United Nations International Children's Education Fund (UNICEF), and Save the Children, to ensure that unaccompanied children are identified and registered, and their families traced.

Stateless Persons

Anne Rose says she has been told that she has no nationality. What does that mean?

Do some research on *statelessness*, looking for information that might apply to the cases of *Kids* Anne Rose and Pang Houa. Then do a role play presenting each of their stories to U.S. government officials who are considering their immigration cases. You can start with this statement by the UNHCR:

> *The right to a nationality is widely recognized in international law... However, as many as nine million people worldwide may remain stateless especially in some countries of the former Soviet Union. The problem is particularly acute among children of parents of mixed origin, or who*

are born in a country other than their parents' country of origin, since they do not necessarily gain citizenship of the place where they are born.

Other Forms of Immigration

The following sections describe some of the many classifications of immigrants designated by the U.S. government and/or international organizations.

Illegal or Undocumented Immigrants

An illegal immigrant is a person who either enters a country illegally, or who enters legally but subsequently violates the terms of their visa, permanent resident permit (green card)or refugee permit. The status and rights of such individuals is a controversial subject that is often linked to economics and moral judgments. There are a number of terms that refer to illegal immigrants. The terms undocumented immigrant and illegals are roughly synonymous, while illegal alien includes those who do not intend to settle in the country, and undocumented worker includes legal residents and even citizens with defective papers who do or do not intend to stay in the country. (http://encyclopedia. laborlawtalk.com/Illegal_immigrant)

 Brainstorm with your club or classmates all the activities you cannot do yet because you are too young, such as drive, drink, go to nightclubs, buy cigarettes, and work full time. Add to that list all the activities you currently do where you had to buy and/or fill out specific documents before you could do them, such as register for school, join a club, travel abroad, get a social security card, or see a doctor. Put each activity on a separate little piece of paper and put all the papers in a hat. Organize a panel of four boys and girls at the front of the room. Each of the others not on the panel picks an activity paper out of the hat and gives it to a panel member. The panel member reads aloud the activity in which the student supposedly engaged without proper documentation and the student must defend himself or herself. The rest of the students vote on what the "jury of peers" proposes as punishment. After the activity, discuss your feelings about the different roles, situations, and judgments and their relationship to immigration.

Trafficked Immigrants

Trafficking in persons is a modern-day form of slavery, involving victims who are typically forced, defrauded, or coerced into sexual or labor exploitation. People generally put themselves or their children in the hands of traffickers to escape poverty and/or discrimination or war. They are promised fantastic opportunities such as well-paid jobs, education, or marriage.

Trafficking in persons is among the fastest growing criminal activities, occurring both worldwide and in individual countries. Annually, at least 600,000–800,000 people, mostly women and children, are trafficked across borders worldwide, including 14,500–17,500 persons into the United States. Trafficked victims do not necessarily enter a country illegally. A trafficker may have arranged legitimate travel documents for the victims.

It is what happens to trafficked victims once they arrive at their destination which distinguishes them from people who migrate or are smuggled into a country illegally. Victims suffer physical and emotional abuse, threats against self and family, passport theft, and physical restraint. (This is based on information at *www.state.gov/g/tip.*)

Federal laws in the United States do not permit any type of slavery. Victims can ask for help, *regardless of immigration status,* using this hotline number: 1-888-373-7888. If you know someone in this situation, please give them this number.

There are many other ways in which people immigrate to the United States, but most of those are not legal. If you are curious about immigration policy and laws, look at the United States Citizenship and Immigrations Services website *(http://uscis.gov)*, the American Immigration Lawyers Association website *(http://www.aila. org)*, as well as other sources listed in the Resources section of this book. These resources will help you to find out more about trafficking, undocumented workers, and proposals for a new U.S. immigration policy. All of these topics would make good research papers.

· ·

Protecting All Migrants/Immigrants

On July 1, 2003, the International Convention on the Protection of the Rights of All Migrant Workers and Members of Their Families entered into force, after being ratified by the required minimum of 20 states in March 2003.

The Convention is a comprehensive international treaty emphasizing the connection between migration and human rights, which is increasingly becoming a crucial policy topic worldwide. The Convention aims at protecting migrant workers; its existence sets a moral standard and serves as a guide and stimulus for the promotion of migrant rights in each country. See the text of this Convention at *www.migrantsrights.org/Int_Conv_ Prot_Rights_MigWorkers_Fam_1999_En.htm.*

As of June 2003, the following countries have ratified this Convention: Azerbaijan, Belize, Bolivia, Bosnia and Herzegovina, Cape Verde, Colombia, Ecuador, Egypt, El Salvador, Ghana, Guatemala, Guinea, Mali, Mexico, Morocco, Philippines, Senegal, Seychelles, Sri Lanka, Tajikistan, Uganda, and Uruguay. (This is based on information from *www.unesco.org/most/migration/convention.*)

See if you can find out why the United States and European countries have not ratified this Convention. Go to *www.unesco.org/most/migration/convention* to find out more about the Convention.

In your class or club, divide into five equal groups of students. Choose an issue that you believe is your right at school, such as the right to wear what you please, the right to state your opinions, and so on. Write a sample "Convention" expressing that right and how to protect it at school. Choose a member of your group to represent you in trying to get other groups to sign your Convention. Make a "fishbowl" circle of representatives from each group at the front of the room. Watch and listen as they present each group's Convention and see which one gets "ratified" first by at least three of the five representatives. Discuss as a large group how and why that happened or didn't!

If you haven't yet, read Kim's story to find out what it's like to live in countries with different laws and rules. If you have lived in another country, what did and didn't you like about it compared to living in the United States? If you have never lived outside of the U.S., what do you imagine it would be like to live and go to school in another country?

Myths and Facts about Immigrants

There are some common misconceptions about immigrants in the United States. Read the sample below from the American Immigration Lawyers Association.

Myth: Immigrants contribute little to American society.

> **Fact:** Besides their significant economic contributions, immigrants continually have helped shape and mold the fabric of our society. Immigrants, for the most part, are firm believers in family unity. They are more likely than natives (U.S.-born persons) to live in families: 76 percent vs. 70 percent. They also tend to have more children: 2.25 vs. 1.93. Immigrants are more likely to be married: 60 percent vs. 55 percent. Only 8 percent of immigrants are divorced or separated compared to 11 percent of natives.
>
> Immigrants recognize the value of an education. While many lack a high school education, they are just as likely as natives to hold a college degree: 20 percent. That rate rose during the 1980s: Among those admitted in 1987–1990, 29 percent held a college degree. Immigrants are also twice as likely as natives to hold Ph.D.'s. Immigrants respect the law as much, if not more, than native born Americans.
>
> They are less likely than natives to be confined to a state prison. Among the five states with the

most immigrants—California, Florida, Illinois, New York, Texas—only New York has a greater share of immigrants in its prisons than in its general population.

So, who are these people we call immigrants?

They could be your parents, your grandparents, your teachers, your friends, your doctors, your policemen, your grocer, your waiter, your cook, your babysitter, your gardener, your lawyer, your favorite actor, actress, or sports hero, your mayor, your congressman or senator, your shopkeeper. Immigrants permeate the fabric of America. They are an integral and important part of our society, its goals and its values. They are the backbone that helps make this country great. They are what set us apart from every nation in this world. In short, they are us.

Reprinted with permission. Copyright © 2005. American Immigration Lawyers Association. *www.aila.org/contect/default.aspx?docid=17242*

Look up the other myths on the website above. Were you taught any of them? Did/do you believe them? Find out why an immigrant can't be president of the United States. Now that you have read the facts, how might you change your behavior toward immigrants? Consider making a poster, writing a poem, having a classroom debate, or creating a play to teach myths and facts about immigrants.

Six of the older *Kids* are already working in the United States: Pang Houa, Tim, Roya, Jina, Jeff, and Jacque. What types of jobs are they doing? How do you think their immigrant experiences might have influenced their choice of career?

· ·

Who Is a U.S. Citizen?

People automatically are U.S. citizens if they are born in any of the 50 U.S. states or if they are children of U.S. citizens. Your birth certificate is proof of your citizenship. People from Puerto Rico, Guam, and the U.S. Virgin Islands also are U.S. citizens. Do you know why that is?

Research the history and current status of Puerto Rico, Guam, and the U.S. Virgin Islands in terms of their relationship to the United States. Have a classroom debate on whether Puerto Rico should keep its status as a U.S. territory, become the 51st state of the U.S., or be an independent country.

· ·

How Do People become U.S. Citizens?

Immigrating to the United States does not make people U.S. citizens. A person may become a U.S. citizen by birth or through naturalization. Non-U.S. citizens go through a process to apply for U.S. citizenship called *naturalization.* In general, you must be at least 18 years old, be a legal resident of the U.S., speak and understand common everyday English, and pass a written test on U.S. history and government. The rest of the requirements and exceptions are outlined on the website *http://uscis. gov/graphics/services/factsheet/howdoi/B3.pdf.*

Could you pass the test to become a citizen? Try a sample of the test and get your score at *http://en carta.msn.com/quiz_14/U_S_Citizenship_Test_Co uld_You_Pass.html.*

People who have one natural or adoptive parent who is a U.S. citizen can themselves become U.S. citizens, like *Kids* Annie and Raoul probably will. U.S. citizens can petition for the following relatives who are abroad to immigrate to the United States; however, they must be able to provide proof of the relationships.

- Husband or wife
- Unmarried child under 21 years old
- Unmarried son or daughter over 21
- Married son or daughter of any age
- Brother or sister, *if the petitioner is at least 21 years old*
- Parent, *if the petitioner is at least 21 years old*

More and more U.S. residents and citizens have been adopting children. They start or expand their families by providing safe, loving homes to children in need. Over 20,000 intercountry adoptions are taking place each year in addition to the more than 200,000 foreign-adopted children already living in the U.S. You can visit the website of the U.S. Citizenship Information Services (USCIS) for more information about how adopted children are brought into the U.S. See *http://uscis.gov/ graphics/services/index2.htm.*

If you or someone you know was adopted in another country and brought to the United States, you should know all the effort that went into making that possible. You can still answer all the questions in this book, either with information about your adoptive family or your birth family or culture—it's up to you. You might also be interested in doing more research into how and why children are adopted from other countries using this website and other sources: *http://uscis.gov/graphics/services/diocase.htm.*

The USCIS website also has information on how to obtain Lawful Permanent Residency (LPR), or green cards. A green card gives you official immigration status—LPR—in the United States. (This is based on information from *http://uscis.gov/graph-ics/services/residency/index.htm.*)

....

Your Family's Immigration/ Migration Story

Do you know when your father's and mother's families came to the United States?

If not, see if you can find out when your family's first members immigrated to the United States and from where. Why did they come to the U.S.? (You might want to look back at the information and questions in the activity Why Do People Leave Their Native Land? earlier in this section. In what part of the U.S. did your family first settle? If you (and your family) need to do some research to answer these questions, try this website: *www.pbs.org/kbyu /ancestors/records/immigration.*

1. If you have Native American Indian heritage, do you know or can you find out the story of your family history and tribe on the North American continent?
2. If you are African American and cannot trace your family back to Africa, how far back can you trace your family's migration within the United States?
3. If you are adopted or part of a blended or multicultural family, you can research the backgrounds of any or all of them!

In many of the stories you have read in this book, the *Kids* refer to "extended" families—those relatives in addition to their parents and siblings. Many of them come from towns or cities where their families have lived for generations, and where they had lots of contact with grandparents, aunts, uncles, and cousins. Extended family members may have been their closest friends, those with whom they attended school and socialized. Some, like Pang Houa, come from a culture where living with multi-generational families of grandparents, parents, and children is the norm. Moving in with relatives in the United States may be the result not only of cultural values, but also because of limited space in urban areas, the need to save money on or look for housing, or because of the loss or absence of an adult family member.

Many Americans also move within the country each year in search of a better life. This mobility separates extended families but contributes to the growth of different parts of the United States. Are there relatives you don't really know because they live far from you? This is an outcome of migration.

Draw a replica of your house. Then draw or find a picture of a U.S. map and a world map and hang them on a wall. You can use these questions as the basis of discussion with your classmates or club members.

1. Draw symbols on your house to show each person who lives there. Do you have any extended family members who live with you? If so, what are the benefits of that and what would you like to change about it if you could?

2. If your extended family is now spread out in different cities, states, or countries, do you know where they are and why that happened?

3. Take a piece of colored string and see if you can trace on the world map the moves that took your family members to their present locations. How many different

towns, states, and countries are represented by family members in your class or club?

4. When and how do you have contact with the relatives who live elsewhere?

Read Jeff's story. In what ways did his brothers influence his life as a newcomer to the United States? If you do or do not have siblings in your house or relatives in your community, how does that affect the ways that you meet people, make friends, and socialize?

Who Lives Where?

You (and your family and teachers) may be surprised at how many nationalities and language groups are represented by the girls and boys in your school, community, and state. Discover this through some of the activities below.

For a math project, have your teacher show you how to use school statistics to create a demographic profile of your school using charts and graphs to show such information as numbers of boys, girls, ages, grade levels, and country or state of origin. Make a bulletin board out of the visuals and see if your school will put it up in the corridor.

Widen this study to include the demographic profile of the entire school district by doing research through the school district offices.

Explore the information provided by the Modern Language Association's (MLA) interactive online tool to discover what languages are spoken in your town/city and state and chart those results. Go to *www.mla.org*.

Develop questions that you and classmates or club members can research on the MLA website, such as: Which state in the United States has the most speakers of Laotian? Which states have the greatest numbers of speakers of others languages? Which have the least? Why?

Look back at all your research findings. What do they show you about where immigrants have settled? Why do you think that is?

· ·

Who Are We?

Explore the cultural heritage of each person in your class or club. Refer to other activities, for example, Meaning of Names and Holidays and Celebrations (in the section Cultures and Customs), and the activity Cultural Diversity/Events (in the section Linking the Classroom to the Community).

Start by having everyone do one or more of the following activities.

1. Create your own personal collage that includes your photo and at least five symbols of things that are important to you about your family and/or culture.
2. Make a mural with all of the collages of your club members or classmates.
3. Put up a U.S. and world map with pins showing where everyone was born.
4. Share your collages and maps with other classes and with your parents, either on back to school night or at a club activity.

Stereotypes, Tolerance, and Diversity

What people from different cultural backgrounds do and believe is the result of their own cultural history, traditions, and experience. When people move into new cultures, they may exhibit different attitudes and behaviors than those of people from the host culture. It is easy to label the way newcomers behave or think as wrong; it is more objective to say that it is *different*.

Differences are generally based on different values or beliefs. For example, young people may be taught not to look into the eyes of an adult. In some cultures, averting the eyes is a sign of respect; looking directly at someone implies that you are an equal or even defiant. We may interpret different behavior incorrectly. Not looking someone in the eyes in the United States may indicate that you are not paying attention or that you are being disrespectful or even dishonest! There is no way to know all of the cultural differences among people, but we can help ourselves and each other to be more open and to watch, listen, and learn.

The activities in this section will help teachers, parents, mentors, and students learn about others, like the *Kids* in this book.

What Are Stereotypes and Why Do We Use Them?

The ability to distinguish friend from foe helped early humans survive, and the ability to quickly and automatically categorize people is a fundamental quality of the human mind. Categories give order to life, and every day we group other people into categories based on social and other characteristics. Catorgorizing, however, also is the foundation of stereotypes, prejudice, and, ultimately, discrimination.

Definition of Terms

A *stereotype* is an exaggerated belief, image, or distorted truth about a person or group—a generalization that allows for little or no individual differences or social variation. Stereotypes are based on images in mass media, or reputations passed on by parents, peers, and other members of society. Stereotypes can be positive or negative.

A *prejudice* is an opinion, prejudgment, or attitude about a group or its individual members. A prejudice can be positive, but in our usage refers to a negative attitude. Prejudices are often accompanied by ignorance, fear, or hatred. Prejudices are formed by a complex psychological process that begins with attachment to a close circle of acquaintances or an "in-group" such as a family. Prejudice is often aimed at "out-groups."

Discrimination is behavior that treats people unequally because of their group memberships. Discriminatory behavior, ranging from slights to hate crimes, often begins with negative stereotypes and prejudices.

from *Teaching Tolerance,* Southern Poverty Law Center, *www.tolerance.org/teach*

1. Can you identify some stereotypes that you have about people from another culture? Where did those stereotypes come from? Find some examples of positive and negative stereotyping in the media and share them with your classmates. How do these examples help shape public opinion? What are *positive stereotypes?* Are they really positive?
2. What stereotypes do you think people from other cultures have about your ethnic, racial or religious group? About Americans? Could any of these stereotypes lead to prejudice? To discrimination? Give some examples. What can you do to help change the attitudes that you and others have about cultures different from your own?

Divide up the stories in the book among small groups. Have each group read their assigned stories and note (1) stereotypes that are raised about the *Kid's* nationality or culture, and (2) stereotypes about Americans that are mentioned in the story. Combine everyone's notes onto a big chart. Discuss each stereotype to determine where or why it might originate, and how it can be helpful or destructive. Discuss how to balance the stereotypes with additional or more accurate information or by reducing the generalization from using the term *all* to *some.*

The following excerpts are from some stories written by a Japanese-American man named Yon when he was in his early 20s. Read these short pieces and then reflect on the questions that follow.

Sansei. Third generation Japanese to live in the United States. A freak. I look Oriental, but my experiences have been completely Western. Not completely. It has been drilled into me over and over again—as if in teaching a retarded child—that I look different from everyone else. Therefore, I couldn't possibly be the same. No one will let me forget that. Individuality is one thing, stereotypical expectations are another. I have become intimately familiar with the subtle distinctions....

I walk through the park watching the squirrels avoid the intrusions of people near their trees. A schoolbus stops on the edge of the road, and several dozen children excitedly run out.. The group gathers around a schoolteacher who tells them to stay within the confines of the park. The children run off in several groups to play.

I continue walking, feeling a light breeze lift my spirits with its fresh piney scents and cooling flutter through my hair. The people in the park seem to belong there, as if existing as part of the scenery, I think. The enjoyment they are obviously experiencing is symbiotically related to the existence of the park. The park needs people to appreciate it, to be concerned with its upkeep and care, to recognize it as a development of love arisen from a formerly tangled mass of weeds and unkempt shrubbery.

A group of young boys from the school group walk past me. They pause to look at me and several of them begin to pull at the corners of their eyes and histrionically chatter nonsensical phrases. They fold their hands as if in prayer and bow to me while narrowing their eyes to slits and protruding their front teeth. They laugh loudly and continue on their way innocently, aware only of the humor they felt.

I stand motionlessly for a time, watching their skipping forms dash off to find new games— games to serve as model experiences for their transitions into adulthood.

I walk home slowly, trying not to feel...

1. What does it mean to be the third generation to live in the United States? What generation are you?
2. According to Yon, does he feel Japanese or American? Why do you think that is?
3. How did Yon's mood change after his encounter with the school boys?
4. How many different stereotypes did the boys in the park have about Japanese people?
5. In addition to his own hurt, what concerns Yon about the experience in the park? Why? What do you think you might have done in Yon's place?
6. How does Yon's description of looking different relate to Jeff's experience in *Kids?*
7. Do some research to find out about Japanese immigration to the United States and the experience of Japanese immigrants during World War II. What do you think

this history might have to do with the stereotypes about Japanese-Americans? Here is a website to start your research: *http://brownvboard.org/brwnqurt/03-4/03-4a.htm.*

Peer Pressure

If you are American-born and between 12 and 21 years old, you might think it's more important to listen to the opinions of and spend time with your peers—people around your own age—than with your family members. Your peers might influence how you dress, what music you prefer, and what you do in your free time. If you live near relatives and have a close-knit family, you may continue to spend time with cousins and other family members. Which is truer for you?

As you read the stories of the *Kids* in the book, many of them describe very strong family ties. Manuel says that his family always got together on weekends and on any holiday in Peru. Jacque found that saying she had a great weekend going to a museum and concert with her family brought looks of surprise from her classmates in the United States. Tim describes the evenings in his town in Kosovo where streets were shut to car traffic and families would walk, talk with friends, stop at cafes, and eat in restaurants. Tim says, "Family and community were very important. We say that days should be spent like this: eight hours working, eight hours sleeping, and eight hours with family." Why might these young people feel differently than you do about spending a lot of time with their families?

Who do you think influences your choices the most: your family, your peers, or yourself for the following?

1. What to wear
2. Who your friends are
3. What you do in your spare time
4. What music you listen to
5. How you wear your hair
6. How much you study
7. Whether you will go to college
8. What type of work you will do after you finish school

Having a strong identification with your peers does not have to mean that you don't have a good relationship with your family. But it is not uncommon for peer groups to do things that are not pleasing to parents: wanting to spend time together rather than with the family, thinking their ideas are "more modern" than their parents' in the choice of music, clothing, films, technology, and social activities.

Peer groups can be very positive in helping young people become more independent, learn to make decisions, and participate in community activities. Peer groups can also become cliques that form strong opinions and exclude anyone different or new. Several of the kids in this book describe difficulty in making friends, and having unpleasant experiences with groups, cliques that did not reach out to welcome newcomers or, worse, were mean or aggressive toward them. Naomi mentions having trouble breaking into cliques, and Jeff describes having to eat alone in the cafeteria as he was not included in any group. Romina describes the unpleasant experience her older brothers had when they were made fun of and called names because of their clothing, and Inayet relays how peers got him in trouble by telling him inappropriate words to use in school.

If you belong to a peer group that is not open to newcomers, what can you do? Role-play how you could respond to such "pressure lines" as the following:

1. "Don't speak to her. She dresses/talks/acts weird."
2. "He doesn't look like us. Look at his hair."
3. "He can't even speak English. How can we talk to him?"
4. "Don't invite her...my parents will kill me and she won't know how we do things."
5. "Why are you going to help her with her homework? Go out with us instead."
6. "Let him be friends with other foreigners or go back where he came from."

If you want to practice some skills to help you make better decisions and become more assertive, do some of the following.

1. Pick one of the *Kid's* stories in this book and think about how you might have approached that young person in order to get to know him or her. How might you have helped the person get adjusted to your school or living in your community? How would you explain to your friends what you want to do?
2. Role-play exercise #1 with a group of your friends. Talk about how your group might reach out to newcomers.
3. Do some of the exercises in the How Does It Feel to Be Different? activity (the next activity) with some of your friends or club members.
4. Find a resource that will help build communication skills, like the *Life Skills Manual* from the Peace Corps (see the online library at *www.peacecorps.org*).

How Does It Feel to Be Different?

Do some of the following exercises to help "feel" what it is like to do common things differently.

1. Put your shoes on the wrong feet. Try to walk.
2. Wear something simple that is unusual for you such as a head cover or scarf around your neck.
3. Visit an "ethnic" grocery store or section of a supermarket and note all the items that are unfamiliar. Check the labels to see where they come from. Try one!
4. Arrange to go to a restaurant that has a menu in another language. Ask if any of the servers speak another language and see if they will teach you how to say in their language the name of the dish you want to order.

Do the language activity "Piglish" to see how it feels to not be able to communicate well and to have to make unfamiliar sounds and gestures. Learn how to tell the story of "The Three Little Pigs" in the pigs' language. (From "New Ways in Teaching Culture," *New Ways in TESOL,* Series II, pp. 65–74). See the Resources section, under Cross-Cultural Classroom Activities.

Do a simulation to learn about different cultures and experience them, such as "The Emperor's Pot" (*Experiential Activities for Intercultural Learning,* Vol. 1, pages 85–99); "Heelotia: A Cross-Cultural Simulation" (SPICE: Stanford Program on International and Cross-cultural Education); or "Rafa Rafa" (for younger children) or "Bafa Bafa" for older students (from Simulation Training Systems). See the Resources section, under Cross-Cultural Classroom Activities.

What Do We Learn from the Media?

The *Kids* in this book come from 23 different countries. Did you know where all those countries are and anything about them before reading their stories? Why or why not? Do the activity below to find out how much you can learn from the media about a country that you choose.

Select a country that you do not know much about. Look for information about that country on TV, in movies, and in the print media (magazines, newspapers, and such).

1. Consider what you find—or do not find. What effect does the media have on what Americans know or think about other countries and cultures?
2. Research other sources that would give you more and better information.
3. Make a one-page newsletter about your chosen country to help inform your club or classmates. Try to find someone who is from that country or has visited there and interview him or her for your newsletter.

Together We Have a Fuller Picture

We know that our perceptions are filtered by many factors: education, values, experiences, and so on. The following are two different activities that will help you see more than one view.

To help you see that your perceptions are not really objective, fill out the following chart. Then compare your answers with a group that isn't just your best friends.

What would you think if...	Your answer	Why?
You saw people dancing in the streets		
A policeman came to the door of your house		
Your parent came to school during a school day		
An older person (stranger) on the bus told you to sit down and be quiet		
You saw someone kill a bird		
A girl asked a boy on a date		
Who would you talk to if...		
You were really sad about something		
You disagreed with the grade your teacher gave you		
You were afraid to ride with your friend who was drunk		
You were angry with a parent		
You heard about a disease and think you have the symptoms		
You don't want to participate in an activity your friends are proposing		

There are more perception activities in the following resources: *Looking at Ourselves and Others,* World Wise Schools, Peace Corps and *Participatory Analysis for Community Action,* Peace Corps. (See the Resources section, under Cross-Cultural Classroom Activities.)

In class or clubs: After completing the preceding activity, do this cooperative map exercise.

Individually sketch a map of the community or a particular section of the city around your school. Only put places on the map that you have visited. Post your maps and walk around looking at them. Discuss what makes the maps different.

1. Are there any important places left off of all the maps? Why?
2. Are there any differences between the girls' maps and the boys' maps or between the maps of students of different backgrounds?
3. Are the maps of longtime residents more detailed than those of newcomers?

Form groups of four or five, take your maps from the wall, and together create a large map that incorporates what each of you had noted individually. After 20 minutes or so of work, post the new maps and walk around and look at them. Discuss the following questions:

1. How are the new maps different from the first ones?
2. What do the maps tell us about exploring other cultures and lifestyles?
3. What does this experience say about working in diverse groups?
4. What has this experience told you about your community?
5. What ideas for individual or group field trips came out of this exercise?
6. What other ideas came from doing this?

Adapted with permission from "The Cooperative Map Exercise," *Experiential Activities for Intercultural Learning,* Vol. 1, pages 133–137.

Linking the Classroom to the Community

The activities in this section are aimed at teachers, facilitators, and club organizers. They provide ways in which schools and clubs can connect to the immigrant experience in the broader community.

All families who move have the same needs to locate housing, groceries, doctors, schools, the post office, and other daily services and all will face some adjustments from where they lived previously. Foreign families may face a maze of totally new systems and may lack the vocabulary to figure them out alone. Consider the confusion of a new secondary school student who is accustomed to spending the entire school day with the same classmates in the same classroom and in the United States has to change classes every hour!

Most communities have systems for helping newcomers. They may have committees to meet and assist families, or they may ask local organizations to do so. Working with new immigrant families can be educational as well as a service; learning should be a two-way street. The extent to which new families feel comfortable and capable to manage their daily needs, and have opportunities to meet people and form friendships, will influence how quickly they can become participating members of the community.

The phrase building bridges *is often used to illustrate the process of bringing culturally diverse groups together. It is certainly necessary to build bridges between communities but true cultural harmony occurs when these bridges are crossed from each side.*

(from *Building and Crossing Bridges: Refugees and Law Enforcement Working Together*, National Crime Prevention Council 1994)

The activities in this section are meant to provide a starting point for getting to know and value immigrant families and to help them become participating members of your community. Your school or club may be doing some of these activities already, but see if there are variations or dimensions that are new for you and your youngsters.

Community Content-Based Instruction

Content based instruction (CBI) is a teaching method that emphasizes learning a language through studying about a subject matter. The Peace Corps used that idea to develop a stronger link to a change-oriented framework and called it *community content-based instruction* (CCBI). In this model, students and their teachers first explore local community issues through field trips, speakers, mapping, and other activities. They then study one or more of those issues at school in the various curriculum areas such as: math (population statistics), science (local ecology), language arts (theater), and social studies (history of the neighborhood). When their exploration is complete, they plan an activity that takes them back to the community to put into action what they have learned. It may be putting on an educational event (play, display, lecture), working on a project (cleaning up a river), starting a campaign (recycling, safety), or other activity to help people improve their lives.

The community garden projects (in the Service Learning activity) are examples of small actions that could come out of CCBI lessons.

The Peace Corps online library/teaching and learning website *(www.peacecorps.gov)* has the CCBI manual and a participant workbook. Both contain sample lesson plans and can be downloaded.

Here is an example of a CCBI lesson plan that includes issues of migration, immigration, and globalization.

1. Interview older individuals in your community about the changes that have taken place there since they were young. See the steps for conducting oral history interviews to help young people in the interview process at *http://score.rims. k12.ca.us/ score_lessons/chavez/ pages/oral-hist_int_ project.html#1.*

2. Create a game for the classroom similar to Simcity (see *http://simcity.ea.com/about/ simcity4/overview.php*) and make it a Sim-countryside. Include an orchard or a crop in your game and introduce agricultural problems and successes. Then introduce industrial growth, trade, and globalization. Take into account prices, culture, weather, and local, national, and international economic factors.

3. Plant a mini-orchard or small crop made of paper in your classroom. Divide the class into groups and make each group responsible for one plant. Have the groups work through simulated situations or difficulties that may arise for growers.

4. As an extension of #3, take another classroom on a tour of your orchard or field. Have the members of the class act as guides, explaining to the other students

about rural life and the changes that have taken place in their orchards or fields over the years.

5. Describe the way your community grew from when it was rural to how it is now. Make maps to describe the changes that might take place in your community over the next few years.

6. Divide the class into groups. Each group will represent a different ethnic group who has been involved in some way in orchard or farming life in your town (local youth, farmers, migrant workers, immigrants). Have each group audiotape or videotape the others as they describe how and why they originally came to your community, what jobs they held and how much they made, what challenges and successes they had, and how things have changed for the worse and for the better in their lives.

7. Compare today's prices of the fruit or crop the class is growing with those of 10 years ago. What are some reasons why the prices are the same or different?

Extensions

1. Students can visit an orchard or farm and document important facets that they observe.

2. Give each student a fruit tree and find a place in the community or school to plant these trees.

3. Get the students involved in obtaining the trees, finding the places to plant them, and caring for the trees.

4. As a class, plan and organize an Arbor Day celebration for your school or community.

Evaluation

Students can be graded on the activity portion of this lesson plan. Evaluate their projects based on whether or not they show understanding of the things that they have learned. Their projects should incorporate an understanding of the history, economics, and ethics of orchards or farms and their growth and their disappearance.

Adapted with permission from the lesson "The Orchard Experience" from the Edpacket page on the website: *http//:sc.lib.byu.edu/events /fruitoflabors/Orchards*)

Service Learning

Service learning is an approach that combines academic instruction, meaningful service, and critical reflective thinking to enhance student learning and civic responsibility. It is a way for young people to explore the concept of the common good and how they can contribute to it. There are various service learning approaches. One model that is available on the web is the World Wise Schools' service learning unit on the Peace Corps website *(www.peacecorps.gov)*, under resources for teachers and students.

There are lessons that can be done with the class or that can be explored by clubs or even individual students or families. They cover (1) the meaning of the common good, (2) how people work for the common good in their community and overseas, (3) how to conduct interviews with community volunteers, (4) learning how service matters to community volunteers, and (5) planning and analyzing the effects of doing a community service project.

To focus a service learning project around immigrants and refugees, you could explore what community volunteers do to assist immigrants and refugees in various ways, including being sponsors, giving free English classes, arranging medical care, helping them access government services, and so on. For example, see the activity Community Resource Guide later in this section. The following are some other examples.

Community Gardens

"Across the country, garden and habitat projects are inspiring students to connect with and serve their communities. They create 'ethnic' plantings that reflect a community's cultures, build intergenerational partnerships, involve neighbors in schoolyard planning, teach citizens about recycling waste, share harvest with populations in need, and create urban oases for respite and renewal.... "

"Connecting to cultures: students explore local food heritage by interviewing families and community members about culturally relevant plants, foods, gardening methods and recipes. They create a garden, visitor's guide, and cookbook reflecting the cultural diversity of the community."

From *Gardens for All* published by the National Gardening Association, Vol. 13, No. 1, Spring 2004, Reprinted with permission by the National Gardening Association, copyright © 2004

. . . .

Global Youth Service Day

Participate in Global Youth Service Day, an annual global event that mobilizes youth and adults to meet the needs of their communities through volunteering, and that helps them learn about and share effective practices in youth service, youth voice, and civic engagement in the world today (see *www.GYSD.net*).

There are some specific activities described later in this section that you may want to engage in: Buddies and Sponsors, Welcoming Activities, Cultural diversity activities/events.

The website for Young People Changing Their World *(www.Dosomething.org)* includes ideas for young people, resources for support, and materials for "community coaches" or adults who want to support young people leading service activities.

Scout troops might want to work toward badges that relate to global issues, social justice, or different cultures. Here are a couple of examples:

- *www.boyscouttrail.com/boy-scouts/ meritbadges/Americanlabor.asp*
- *www.girlscouts.org/program/gs_ central/insignia/online/junior/world_ in_my_community.asp*

Also see the Resources section for many club references.

Living in a Global World

Sometimes we forget that every day we are linked with other countries, from the foods we eat to the clothes we wear and the music we listen to. Create an ongoing series of explorations that tie the world together.

Favorite Foods: See the Foods activity in the section Cultures and Customs.

Clothes: Where are they made? Have everyone check the tags on all the clothes they are wearing one day and locate on a world map where they were made or assembled. If age appropriate, research the globalization of the garment industry and the opportunities and constraints that it has produced. Look up the rights of children and the efforts to prevent and end child labor (see the UN International Programme on the Elimination of Child Labour at *www.ilocarib.org.tt/clmis_web/clmis.htm*). Also see what United Students Against Sweatshops is doing to help eliminate child labor *(www.studentsagainstsweatshops.org)*.

Sports: Explore the sports played by students or American athletes on TV. Where did those sports originate? In what countries are they currently played? How do sports get introduced into other countries? The following are some sample questions.

1. How did baseball get spread around the world from the United States? What countries do some of the players in the U.S. baseball leagues come from? Find out more about the history of baseball in one of your favorite player's country.
2. Investigate the Michigan Cricket Association: Who started it? When? Who plays? How is it being adapted to become more accepted in the United States?
3. Research how and why players from all over the world now play on U.S. sports teams and vice versa.

Music: Have students name their favorite Latin music performers. Find out the countries of origin for each singer/group. Listen to several types of Latin music and find out the countries of origin for each one of those (see *www.putamayo.com*).

The following are some discussion or research questions.

1. How are the performers and the music the same or different?
2. Why might that be?
3. Which ones have had the greatest influence on American music and why?

Simulation: Try doing the simulation "Living in a Global Age" to help students understand global resources, interdependence, and the need for global negotiations and diplomacy. The simulation is available from SPICE: Stanford Program on International and Cross-cultural Education at *http://spice.stanford.edu.*

....

Buddies and Sponsors

Sponsors (sometimes called *community volunteers*) are individuals or families who agree to meet and work with newcomers to help them get settled. They often visit the home, drive people around to help them get their bearings, provide temporary transportation, and introduce the new family to schools and services. The following are some variations on sponsors.

• Having more than one sponsor. One sponsor may help with general community orientation and getting settled. Another family may be selected because they have children of the same age as the children in the family. Each member of the family assists in getting their counterpart familiar with relevant activities and is available to answer questions.

- A *buddy* is someone of the same age as each school-age child in the new family. These young sponsors can take the children to age-appropriate activities to meet others, get an idea of how children their age dress, and help them get to and around school for a few weeks. Many foreign families are used to extended families for support and friendship, and they may be surprised how age-segmented activities often are in U.S. communities.

Explore what agencies or organizations assist new-comers in your community. Find out if your class or club could help with sponsoring new families.

Welcoming Activities

Providing an informal way for families to meet people in the community can be very welcoming. This is particularly important for families with children who arrive during the summer when school is out and many people may be taking vacations. The following are some variations.

- One or more sponsors of new families can put on a small event for the families they are sponsoring. The guests may include neighbors and families with children of the same age.
- Prior to the beginning of school, it is useful for families to come together so new families can meet others and their children can make some acquaintances before school starts. If such an event can be held at the school, it might also include a tour of the school.

Have students interview the administration of your school to find out what activities are planned for newcomers. If appropriate, see if your class or club can be part of these activities, or create some new ones that they think will be helpful.

Linking Newcomers to Institutions and Clubs

Members of any organized group or club can invite new community members to a meeting, activity, or event to introduce them to the organization and to new people. Immigrant families may be unfamiliar with the way clubs and sports are organized in the United States, and having the opportunity to visit may provide an opening for them to make friends or find an activity they like. Studies have shown that newcomers adapt the quickest to their new culture if they can find at least one local activity they enjoy and can participate in.

1. Groups can develop *buddy programs* that reach out to newcomers and assist them with homework or other needs. Find out if such a program exists in your community or school. If not, see if there are students who would like to form such a group.
2. Many community groups (adult and youth) have service projects or particular learning requirements (such as Scouts). Projects involving newly arrived immigrant families may be a good fit for your club or group. (See the Resources section, under Youth Club/Programs for ideas)

Language Help

Children will learn at school and will be helped by making American friends with whom to play and converse. They usually pick up language fairly quickly, especially if they have English-speaking friends. Adults may find it harder to learn functional language, especially those who are not in work-places.

Consider if your school, PTA, or club might like to help coordinate some of the following for new immigrants:

1. Conversation groups or classes at a convenient time for stay-at-home adults.
2. Including them in clubs and activities where they will hear and use language; as needed, provide a buddy to help explain things.
3. Involving adults in meaningful activities where they will be in contact with English speakers regularly, such as helping with child care or preschool, after-school programs for children, sports teams, scouts, or other groups. Links through these activities are often the ways newcomers begin to feel a part of their new culture.

Cultural Diversity Activities/Events

Communities and schools sponsor food and craft fairs, talent shows, and other events that provide opportunities to learn about the various cultures in their neighborhood. In addition to celebrating typical U.S. holidays, non-U.S. holidays can also be addressed through programs that feature information, food, and rituals/dances.

The following are some other types of events that you and your students, PTAs, or club members might consider doing or coordinating.

1. Films, panels, and guest speakers as part of an ongoing educational series that shares the cultural diversity of the community.

2. Families who are new to the community may benefit from a meeting where students or families who have lived there for five years or less talk about their adjustment issues, ways of adapting, and how to become involved in community life. (See *Experiential Activities for Intercultural Learning,* Vol. 1, pp. 139–141.)

3. Cooking classes that feature food from different cultures represented in the community are a good way to introduce new tastes and new community members.

4. Businesses can provide shadow days, take children to work days, or internships that involve both immigrant and American children, making intergenerational contacts as well as sharing information about different types of work.

Community Resource Guide

The International Center of Indianapolis *(www. icenterindy.org),* in conjunction with Bridges to the World: Connecting Youth Around the Globe activities, produced an attractive accordion leaflet entitled *Know the World in Your Backyard.*

Dedicated "to building relationships and learning from new neighbors from many different countries," it encourages families to experience and learn in their own neighborhoods. There are sections on joining in holiday celebrations; getting involved in different educational or support organizations; worshipping with a different religious group; listening and learning opportunities for movies, plays, musical presentations, and TV and radio stations; attending or participating in different sports; visiting ethnic grocery stores and restaurants; exploring other cultures through their literature (both children's and adult); and learning a language or assisting second-language learners. For each topic there is a list of local possibilities.

Could you do one of the above in your community? Any of these would be great activities for pairing-up classes, schools, PTAs, scout troops, or other clubs from different neighborhoods.

Activities for Various Audiences

Many of the activities can be used by various kinds of groups with little or no modification. After the description of an activity, modifications for different audiences are suggested, as needed. The following chart should help you locate activities for your particular situation.

AUDIENCE

ACTIVITIES		Individuals	Classes	Schools	PTAs	Clubs	Families	Communities
	Cultures and Customs							
	Meaning of Names	✓	✓			✓	✓	
	Friendship	✓	✓			✓	✓	
	Holidays and Celebrations	✓	✓	✓	✓	✓	✓	✓

AUDIENCE

	Indivi-duals	Classes	Schools	PTAs	Clubs	Fami-lies	Commu-nities
Religion	✓	✓	✓		✓	✓	
Map of Your House	✓	✓			✓	✓	
Public and Private Behaviors and Topics of Conversation	✓	✓			✓	✓	
Family Rules	✓	✓			✓	✓	
Pets	✓	✓			✓	✓	
Foods	✓	✓	✓	✓	✓	✓	✓
Routines and Rituals	✓	✓			✓	✓	
Values and Behaviors	✓	✓	✓		✓	✓	
Schools	✓	✓	✓		✓	✓	
Write Your Own Story	✓	✓	✓	✓	✓		
Interview Someone	✓	✓	✓	✓	✓	✓	✓
Immigration and Citizenship							
We Are All Immigrants	✓	✓	✓	✓	✓	✓	
Who Is Coming to the U.S. Now?	✓	✓	✓	✓	✓	✓	

ACTIVITIES

AUDIENCE

ACTIVITIES		Individuals	Classes	Schools	PTAs	Clubs	Families	Communities
	Why Do People Leave Their Native Land?	✓	✓	✓		✓	✓	
	Protecting All Migrants/ Immigrants	✓	✓	✓		✓	✓	
	Myths and Facts about Immigrants	✓	✓	✓	✓	✓	✓	
	Who Is a U.S. Citizen?	✓	✓	✓		✓	✓	
	How Do People Become U.S. Citizens?	✓	✓	✓		✓	✓	
	Your Family's Immigration/ Migration Story	✓	✓	✓	✓	✓	✓	✓
	Who Lives Where?	✓	✓	✓		✓	✓	✓
	Who Are We?	✓	✓	✓	✓	✓	✓	✓
	Stereotypes, Tolerance, and Diversity							
	What Are Stereotypes and Why Do We Use Them?	✓	✓			✓	✓	
	Peer Pressure	✓	✓	✓		✓		
	How Does It Feel to Be Different?	✓	✓	✓		✓	✓	
	What We Learn from the Media	✓	✓	✓		✓		
	Together We Have a Fuller Picture	✓	✓	✓		✓		✓

AUDIENCE

ACTIVITIES	Indivi-duals	Classes	Schools	PTAs	Clubs	Families	Communities
Linking the Classroom to the Community							
Community Content-Based Instruction	✓	✓	✓		✓	✓	
Service Learning	✓	✓	✓		✓	✓	✓
Living in a Global World	✓	✓	✓	✓	✓	✓	
Buddies and Sponsors	✓	✓	✓	✓	✓	✓	✓
Welcoming Activities		✓	✓	✓	✓	✓	✓
Linking Newcomers to Institutions and Clubs	✓	✓	✓	✓	✓	✓	✓
Language Help	✓	✓	✓	✓	✓	✓	✓
Cultural Diversity Activities/Events		✓	✓	✓	✓		✓
Community Resource Guide		✓	✓	✓	✓		✓

Resources

This section contains many of our favorite resources as well as links to additional information. It is definitely suggestive, not exhaustive. Note: the authors looked at every website we have listed and tried to get balanced ones, but we can't guarantee the accuracy of the information on each site or that it will still be available when you are reading this book. The sites do not necessarily represent our views or those of our publisher. If websites are no longer accurate, try locating the organization on the web first. Then follow its links to materials.

Cross-Cultural Classroom Activities

Experiential Activities for Intercultural Learning, Vol.1. H. Ned Seelye, ed. Intercultural Press: Boston. 1996. This volume focuses on the development of intercultural awareness and cross-cultural sensitivity. It has activities that vary in complexity and can be used or adapted for various age groups.

New Ways in Teaching Culture. Alvino E. Fantini, ed. Teachers of English to Speakers of Other Languages (TESOL), Alexandria, VA. 1997. *www.tesol.org.* This volume provides background and activities that explore how language, culture, and intercultural work belong together. Activities at various levels.

The Peace Corps, 1111 20th Street, NW, Washington, DC 20026. *www.peacecorps.gov*

World Wise Schools is an office of the Peace Corps that links Peace Corps volunteers with classrooms and provides materials to classrooms. Some resources for teachers are:

1. *Looking at Ourselves and Others* and *The Bridge* are two good general sources for cross-cultural activities for the classroom.
2. *Voices from the Field* and *Uncommon Journeys* provide short stories written by Peace Corps volunteers with lesson plans for the classroom based on them. Many good ideas for teachers on how to use the stories for broader learning. Lesson plans indicate related standards.
3. A service learning module of session plans can be accessed on the site. From the Peace Corps website, click on materials for teachers and students to reach World Wise Schools.

The online library on the website has many other downloadable Peace Corps resources. The following are particularly relevant to classrooms:

1. *Culture Matters*—Cultural concepts with activities.
2. *Life Skills*—Session plans for students to develop good skills for becoming thoughtful and competent adults; several sections, including one on peer pressure, are useful when facing cultural differences in the classroom.
3. *Community Content-Based Instruction*—Shows how school curriculum can be linked to community issues, and students can do community projects to reinforce their classroom learning.

Working with Youth: Approaches for Volunteers— Provides key ideas on positive youth development, youth participation, and asset-based community development. The many youth activities shared in the books are linked to Search Institute *(www.search-institute.org)*. Asset types of support include empowerment, boundaries and expectations, constructive use of time, commitment to learning, positive values, social competencies, and positive identities.

Stanford Programs on Intercultural and Cross-cultural Education (SPICE) outreach center at Stanford University *(http://spice.stanford.edu)* has various simulations and units, for example "Heelotia: A Cross-cultural Simulation" and "Living in a Global Age" simulation, and classroom units on "Why Do People Move? Migration from Latin America," and "Historical Legacies: The Vietnamese Refugee Experience." Sessions are referenced to national standards for social studies, geography, and so on.

Simulation Training Systems *(www.simulation trainingsystems.com)* produces experiential learning modules for various audiences. "Rafa Rafa" (for younger students) and "Bafa Bafa" (for older students and adults) are simulations that quickly put participants into different cultures where they must behave according to cultural norms, as well as interact with yet a different culture.

Teaching Tolerance magazine, published by the Southern Poverty Law Center, a nonprofit legal and education foundation, contains classroom activities submitted by teachers. Mailed twice a year at no charge to educators. Can be accessed through its website: *www.teaching tolerance.org*

All Human Beings—A Manual for Human Rights Education from The Teacher's Library, UNESCO publishing, 1998. This resource introduces both an approach and method for human rights education, and contains sessions for teaching human rights in the classroom.

On the Cyberschoolbus website *(www.un.org/cyber schoolbus)*, teachers can find lesson plans on global issues and publications for grades K–12. Students can participate in finding solutions to global problems. Country profiles, including region and country maps, an introduction to the UN, a kid-friendly version of human rights principles, Model UN support, interactive games, and more. Students can, for example, pick up to six countries and develop bar graphs showing comparative statistics about population, health, environment, and so on.

The New Americans website offers an online educational adventure for 7th–12th grade students. The site supplements the upcoming documentary miniseries, which explores the immigrant experience through the personal stories of immigrants to the United States. *www.pbs.org/independentlens/newamericans* *The New Americans* Series Guide and Activity Kit for higher-education settings, including ESOL and professional development, is available through the Community Connections Project at *www.itvs.org.*

For grades 7–12, interactive sections provide users with opportunities to explore the immigration experience interactively—through a timeline, maps, and exercises in tracking family history and examining the effect of immigration on the nation.

The "For Educators" section of this site offers 11 lesson plans that address varied historic and modern-day immigration issues. Lesson plans aligned with national academic performance standards give students hands-on opportunities to grasp the essence of immigration to the United States, from analyzing factual data to conducting oral histories of first- or second-generation immigrants.

Video/Film
Maria Full of Grace—This is a great film for classroom discussions. Catalina Sandino Moreno's film debut won

her a 2004 Academy Award nomination for Best Actress. Her portrayal of a 17-year-old village girl from Colombia provides Americans with some of the most insightful answers to the questions of illegal immigration and drug trafficking.

Teens in Between—This 84-minute documentary follows five recent immigrant teenagers through a year in their lives at Annandale High School in northern Virginia. A complete educational resource guide is now available free of charge at *www.mbznetworks.org/teensin between*. There are activities and discussion guides for English and Social Studies classes (Grades 7–Adult), English as a Second Language classes (ESL Grades 9–Adult), and Staff Training and Development.

"Teen Immigrants: 5 American Stories" in "In the Mix, the PBS Teen Series" which has video clips, transcript, and discussion guide. Find at *www.inthemix.org*

Community Outreach

Bridges to the World: Connecting Youth Around the Globe, International Center of Indianapolis *(www.icenter indy.org)*. This is an example of a community center committed to improving intercultural interactions. Good sample programs and materials. Illusion Theater creates theater that illuminates the human condition by addressing the illusions, myths, and realities of our times. Illusion uses the power of theater to be a catalyst for

personal and social change through its mainstage productions as well as its education and outreach presentations. Illusion is nationally known for producing original work by living, breathing artists, including the annual Fresh Ink series, which features a new play every week during the summer season. One of their productions, *Undesirable Elements,* is similar to the readers' theater suggestion for using stories in this book (see the activity Interview Someone in the Cultures and Customs section). See *www.illusiontheater.org*

Resources on Immigrant Groups

There are descriptions of various immigrant groups on the Library of Congress website at *http://memory.loc.gov/learn/features/immig/introduction2.html.*

Native Americans

Native Village Youth and Education News, a free newsletter which informs and celebrates in the education, values, traditions, and accomplishments of the Americas' First Peoples. *www.nativevillage.org*

Nihewan Foundation for Native American Education, a nonprofit organization dedicated to more accurate curriculum about Native Americans, including the Cradleboard Teaching Project. *www.nihewan.org*

Library of Congress website on Native Americans as the first "immigrants" to the Americas whose ancestors virtually were "destroyed by the subsequent immigration that created the United States. This tragedy is the direct result of treaties, written and broken by foreign governments, of warfare, and of forced assimilation." *http://memory.loc.gov/learn/features/immig/native_american.html*

African Americans

Learn about the early Black explorers in the Americas at: *http://www.britannica.com/ebi/article-197662*

PBS print resources for kids on the topic of slavery in the United States: *www.pbs.org/wnet/slavery/resources /kids.html*

National Endowment for the Humanities sample lesson plans for different grade levels using real slave narratives describing their "immigration" and lives: *http://edsite ment.neh.gov/view_ lesson_ plan.asp?id=364*

Amnesty International Human Rights lesson plans on slavery: *www.amnestyusa.org/education/lessonplans /article4.html*

The Immigration Story—Individual States

Arkansas: *www.arkansasheritage.com/people_stories/*

"The people of Arkansas are as wonderfully diverse as the varied landscapes on which they settled. Even today, the population of Arkansas reflects the ethnic diversity of the immigrants who centuries ago traveled from around the world to settle here."

Virginia: Becoming Americans: Our Struggle to Be Both Free and Equal is a plan of thematic interpretation at Colonial Williamsburg in Virginia. The book, which reflects historical interpretation in the reconstructed capital of the Virginia colony, covers such topics as "Enslaving Virginia," "Redefining Family," "Choosing Revolution," and "Freeing Religion." It deals with white settlers of various classes, free and slave blacks, and Native Americans. Materials and programs are available through *www.history.org/history/teaching/tchcrone.cfm* and *www.history.org/history/teaching/classroom_ plans.cfm*

Immigration, General

Modern Language Association interactive online language map of the United States, based on 2000 U.S. census data: *www.mla.org*

Human Development Reports. For more mature students, and for research and understanding statistics, these reports can provide an understanding of why some people immigrate for better opportunities in the U.S. *http://hdr.undp.org*

United Nations High Commission on Refugees: *www. unhcr.org.* The Office of the United Nations High Commissioner for Refugees was established on December 14, 1950 by the United Nations General Assembly. The agency is mandated to lead and coordinate international action to protect refugees and resolve refugee problems worldwide. Its primary purpose is to safeguard the rights and well-being of refugees. It strives to ensure that everyone can exercise the right to seek asylum and find safe refuge in another country, with the option to return home voluntarily, integrate locally, or to resettle in a third country.

American Immigration Lawyers Association website on immigration myths: *www.aila.org/contect/default.aspx? docid=17242* Article about civics and voting rights for immigrants by Michele Wucker, 2003: *www.aflcio. org/issuespolitics/immigration/upload/Civics-Lessons-from-Immigrants.pdf*

Library of Congress website with interactive online quizzes, including one for Spanish words in the English language, Native American geography, Irish sayings, etc.: *http://memory. loc.gov/learn/features/immig/ vocabulary.html*

Library of Congress resources on immigration: *http://memory.loc.gov/learn/features/immig/interv/resources.html*

Library of Congress interactive online immigrant recipe book: *http://memory.loc.gov/learn/features/immig/ckbk/index.html*

Comprehensive materials on U.S. immigration history and policy from the Close-Up Foundation: *www.closeup.org/immigrat.htm #overview* and *www.closeup.org/immi_act.htm*

Other Sources

www.migrationinformation.org/GlobalData/countryda ta/data.cfm

www.pbs.org/teachersource/thismonth/mar04/index1.s htm

Two sites from multicultural educator and author Paul Gorski:

1. The Multicultural Pavilion *(www.edchange.org/multicultural)* was created in 1995 to provide resources for educators, students, and activists to explore and discuss multicultural education; facilitate opportunities for educators to work toward self-awareness and development; and provide forums for educators to interact and collaborate toward a critical, transformative approach to multicultural education.

2. Transformations Book Store is a browsing space for books, films (both DVD and VHS), journals, and magazines related to equity, peace, social justice, and progressive education. Transformations is a resource

of *http://EdChange.org* and the Multicultural Pavilion.

Refugees

Web Resources

ReliefWeb serves the informational needs of humanitarian relief community: *www.reliefweb.int*

Immigration and Refugee Services of America: *www.refugeesusa.org*

Office of Refugee Resettlement, Administration for Children and Families is a federal agency that funds state, territory, local, and tribal organizations: *www.acf.hhs.gov/ programs/orr*

Center for Immigration Studies: *www.cis.org*

University of Minnesota Human Rights Library: *www.umn.edu/humanrts/links*

Building and Crossing Bridges: Refugees and Law Enforcement, National Crime Prevention Council, Series BJA, July 1994: *www.ncpc.org*

Service Learning: Web Resources

Peace Corps: *www.peacecorps.gov*

Community Outreach and Partnerships in Service-Learning, Indiana University: *www.indiana.edu/~copsl*

Corporation for National and Community Service; includes National Service Learning Clearinghouse: *www.nationalservice resources.org*

Youth Service America. Provides a link to its toolkit, Project Plan-It!, an online planning and implementation guide for young people. The toolkit also includes useful tip sheets, such as how to recruit volunteers or develop resources. *www.ysa.org/planit*

Learn & Serve. Part of the Corporation for National Community Service (listed earlier). One useful resource located here is the guidebook, *Students in Service to America Guidebook,* which is a great primer on service learning. *www.learnandserve.org*

Points of Light Foundation. Has many ready-to-use service tools, including "Service Project Ideas for Youth" and "Planning a One-Day Volunteer Event." You must create a login ID to access their materials, but they are free. *www.pointsoflight.org*

City Year & National Youth Corps. "An Action Tank for national service, City Year seeks to demonstrate, improve and promote the concept of national service as a means for building a stronger democracy. An 'action tank' is both a program and a 'think tank' —constantly combining theory and practice to advance new policy ideas, make programmatic breakthroughs, and bring about major changes in society." *www.city-year.org/about/index.cfm*

YouthBuild USA. Young people provide service in their communities through construction or rehabilitation of homes and training youth to serve as community and organizational leaders. *www.youthbuild.org*

America's Promise, the Alliance for Youth—Power of Five. Provides facilitator tools and worksheets for those

11-14 to build leadership skills and build character. *www.americaspromise.org/poweroffive*

National Youth Leadership Council. Provides innovative examples of service activities, new types of partnerships, and programs that are replicable and promising. *www.nylc.org*

DoSomething.Org. Includes ideas for young people, resources for support, and materials for "community coaches" or adults who want to support young people leading service activities. *www.Dosomething.org.*
Center for Youth as Resources. "Young people from all walks of life taking the lead in community change." Includes resources on violence prevention, environmental action, and civic engagement. *www.YAR.org*

National Gardening Association. Their mission is to sustain and renew the fundamental links between people, plants, and the earth, and produce a magazine, *Gardens for All,* which reports on and encourages student projects that build links with the community. Vol 13, No. Spring 2004 focuses on service learning, and has stories of intercultural cooperation and projects: *www.garden.org.* It has grant programs for schools through *www.kids gardening.com*

U.S. School Standards

National Social Studies Standards: *www.socialstudies. org/standards*

National Geography Standards: *www.ncge.org/standard*

ACTFLD foreign language standards: *www.act fl.org/i4a/pages/index.cfm?pageid=3324*

English as a Second Language (ESL) standards:
www.cal.org/eslstandards

Youth Clubs/Programs

Girl Scouts *(www.girlscouts.org)* goals include to "develop a meaningful set of values to guide their actions and provide for sound decision-making and contribute to the improvement of society." Two program areas the scouts can work on are leadership and self-esteem, and community outreach and education. They also have "The World in My Community" badge. (Many similar activities as those in this book.)

Boy Scouts *(http://usscouts.org)* has several relevant programs and badges: "Heritages" and "Language and Culture" academic programs; "Citizenship in the Community" and "American Cultures" merit badges.

Boys and Girls Clubs *(www.bgca.org)*. "Club programs and service promote and enhance the development of boys and girls by instilling a sense of competence, usefulness, belonging and influence;" programs in character and leadership, education and career, as well as specialized activities such as youth for unity; and "a diversity education program designed to combat prejudice, bigotry and discrimination."

The following is a sample of other groups with special youth programs.

Red Cross youth programs. Youth are involved in almost every aspect of the American Red Cross. The American Red Cross offers youth, age 18 and younger, many opportunities in community service and volunteerism. Red Cross youth respond to disasters, provide education to their peers and other community members on how to stay safe, and support Red Cross blood drives through recruiting blood donors and sponsoring blood drives. As peer educators, youth teach members of their community about water safety, CPR and first aid, community disaster education, HIV/AIDS, international humanitarian law, and baby sitting. *www.redcross.org/services/youth/0,1082,0_326_,00.html*

Kiwanis. K-Kids in elementary schools, Builders Clubs in middle schools, Key clubs in high schools, and Circle K International in colleges are service organizations whose members are dedicated to improve their schools and communities. Virtually any unanswered need is a potential opportunity for commitment and dedication.

- *www.kkids.org/kkids/about* for K-Kids Clubs
- *www.buildersclub.org/builders/about/ faq.asp* for Builders Clubs
- *www.keyclub.org/keyclub/about/faq.asp* for Key Clubs
- *www.circlek.org/circlek/about/faq.asp* for Circle K International

Rotary International exchange programs: *www.rotary.org /programs/youth_ex/history.html*

Optimists—Junior Optimists Octagon International (JOOI). 17,600 members in 690 clubs throughout the United States, Canada, the Caribbean, and France, making their communities better—one service project at a time. The numbers are increasing all the time, thanks in part to visionary educators who recognize the desire that so many kids have to help other kids in their community. *www.junioroptimists.org*

Pilot International. Anchor Clubs allow young people to make a difference in their world through volunteer service and by learning valuable skills that prepare them to be good citizens for the rest of their lives, including opportunities to lead and organize service projects and play active roles in club programs. Anchor members discover the importance of working together—no single member can accomplish the service that the members can as a team. *www.pilotinternational.org/html/ anchor/anchor.shtml*

Lions Club. The mission of Lions Opportunities for Youth is to provide the young people of the world with opportunities for achievement, learning, contribution, and service, individually and collectively, through sponsorship of activities identified as best practices in the field of youth development. Opportunities include Lions Youth Outreach Program and Leo Club Youth Programs. Leos learn how to become involved in their communities, help their neighbors, and serve as community leaders.

- *www.lionsclubs.org/EN/content/youth_ index.shtml*
- *www.lionsclubs.org/EN/content/youth_leo_ clubs.shtml*

Multicultural Education

This section includes a compilation of some useful resources, materials, and websites on topics related to multicultural education.

EmTech is a site with over 15,000 Internet resources organized by topics for teachers, students, and parents. This URL takes you right to the multicultural resources. *http://www.emtech.net/multicultural_education.html#L atino%20and%20Hispanic.*

This site has lesson plans in multiple subject areas including PE, foreign language, technology, as well as core

subjects. *http://www.education-world.com/preservice/
learning/multicultural.shtml*

Multicultural topics include a new lesson called "Looking
at..." can help teachers integrate global education into the
classroom. *http://jan.ucc.nau.edu/~jar/Multi.html*

Grade-level and standards-based lesson plans on
immigration from the American Immigration Law
Foundation: *http://www.ailf.org/pubed/tc_lessonplans.
asp#TENTH*

Southern Poverty Law Center materials on overcoming
bias and discrimination, conflict resolution, etc.
www.tolerance.org/teach

The Multicultural Pavilion includes Teacher's Corner,
Multicultural Awareness Archives, an Online Discussion
Board, and many other "departments." The Teacher's
Corner has "resources for teachers, including reviews of
children's music, multicultural activities, and online
literature archives." *www.edchange.org/multicultural*

Varieties of Multicultural Education: An Introduction, an
ERIC Digest article by Gary Burnett, discusses the
controversy and policy debate regarding multicultural
education; provides research links; and outlines
"typologies of multicultural education." *www.ericdigests.
org/1995-1/multicultural.htm*
This collection of Northwest Regional Educational
Laboratory (NWREL) resources focuses on
multicultural education. The suggested approach is to
view multicultural education as a perspective that is
integrated into the daily activities of the classroom. If it
begins with teachers' self-reflection, it also includes an
examination of the racism and biased attitudes and
behaviors that are structured into our society and our
schools, and an exploration and validation of the many

cultures that make up the classroom, our nation and our world. From Beyond Family Involvement: School-Based Child and Family Support Programs. *www.nwrel.org/comm/topics/multicultural.html*

The Multicultural Education Internet Resource Guide has over 100 websites created to assist multicultural educators in locating educational resources on the Internet. *http://jan.ucc.nau. edu/~jar/Multi.html*

Multicultural art—the largest collection of free art lessons on the Internet, including how to make objects from different cultures out of everyday household materials. *http://kinderart. com/multic*

A compilation of lesson plans with a multicultural focus for teachers (K–12) that target multicultural education, as well as lesson plans for other subjects.*wwwlibrary. csustan. edu/lboyer/multicultural/lesson2.htm*

Links to thousands of resources, papers, lesson plans, and projects in multicultural education. *www.awe somelibrary.org/Classroom/Social_ Studies/ Multicultural/Multicultural.html*

University of West Florida Library bibliography on multicultural education. *www.lib.uwf.edu/ eli/Education/multicultural_education.shtml*

Links to lesson plans about multicultural education that could be useful in implementing multicultural ideas into your classroom. *www.geocities.com*

"A Synthesis of Scholarship in Multicultural Education" (1994). A comprehensive yet concise explanation of multicultural education by Geneva Gay, Ph.D., professor of education and faculty associate of the Center for

Multicultural Education at the University of Washington-Seattle. *www.ncrel.org/sdrs/areas/ issues/educatrs/ leadrshp/le0gay.htm*

Clearly written piece for teachers on the advantages and limitations of the concept of cultural learning styles. *www.ncrel.org/sdrs/areas/issues/educatrs/presrvce/ pe3lk10.htm*

National Character Education Center: Character Education Program For Schools. This program is teaching character in over 5,000 schools worldwide. This is a great site for multicultural/ character education or both. It has lesson plans that are cross-curricular and include writing activities. *www.ethicsusa.com*

Lessons in Peace, Diversity, and Social Change

Global Village School: Lessons in Peace, Diversity, and Social Change. *www.newhorizons.org/strategies/ multicultural/chandler.htm*

Selected Readings

The five readings you will find at the websites below provide background and perspectives on culture, migration, and globalization. The readings may be useful to older students and to teachers, parents and mentors.

1. *Migration and Globalization: www.icftu. org/displaydocument.asp?Index=9909 16306& Language=EN*
2. *Migrating in Search of Farmwork:* from Fields Without Borders. Student Action with Farmworkers,

1999 *http://cds.aas.duke.edu/saf/article migrating.htm*
3. *Lives in Limbo* by Marina Budhos: *http://www. marinabudhos.com*
4. *On Becoming American:An Exploratory Essay* by Sonia Nieto: *http://store. tcpress.com/0807737208. shtml#299*
5. *Hispanic, Latino or Chicano? A Historical Review* by Frank del Olmo: *http://www.nahj.org/resource guide/intro2.html*

Literature

Books about Young Immigrants for Secondary School Students

This list was compiled by the authors and *http://www.iso media.com/homes/jmele/joe.html; http://www.btpl.org /Youth_Services/Youth_Books/Youth_Immigration_Bib/you th_immigration_bib.html;* and *http://centerforlearning.org*

ASIAN-AMERICAN AND PACIFIC ISLANDER

Crew, Linda. *Children of the River.* 1989. (Cambodian)
Lee, Gus. *Honor and Duty.*1994. (Chinese)
Lee, Marie. *Finding my Voice.*1992. (Korean-American)
Mak, Kam. *My Chinatown.*1997. (Hong Kong Chinese)
Na, An. *A Step from Heaven.* 2001. (Korean)
Say, Allen. *Grandfather's Journey.* 1993. (Japanese)
Whelan, Gloria. *Goodbye Vietnam.* 1992. (Vietnamese)

LATIN AMERICAN

Alvarez, Julia. *How the Garcia Girls Lost Their Accents.* 1991.
(Dominican)
Bernardo, Anilu. *Fitting In.* 1996. (Cuban)

Buss, Fran Leeper, and Daisy Cubias. *Journey of the Sparrows.* 1991. (Salvadoran)

Lachtman, Ofelia. *The Girl from Playa Blanca.* 1995. (Mexican)

Soto, Gary. *Local News.* 1993. (Mexican)

Stanek, Muriel. *I Speak English for My Mom.* 1989. (Mexican)

MIDDLE EASTERN AND SOUTH ASIAN

Chopra, Prem N. *Salaam New York.* 1993. (Indian)

Dumas, Firoozeh. *Funny in Farsi: A Memoir of Growing Up Iranian in America.* 2003. (Iranian)

Laird, Elizabeth. *Kiss the Dust.* 1991. (Iraqi)

Nye, Naomi Shihab. *Habibi.* 1997. (Palestinian-American)

Staples, Suzanne Fisher. *Haveli.* 1993. (Pakistani)

CARIBBEAN

Hanson, Regina. *The Tangerine Tree.* 1995. (Jamaican)

AFRICAN

Mathabane, Mark. *Kaffir Boy in America.* 1989. (South African)

EUROPEAN

Armstrong, Jennifer. *Lili the Brave.* 1997. (Norwegian)

Auch, Mary Jane. *Ashes of Roses.* 2002. (Irish)

Durbin, William. *The Journal of Otto Peltonen: A Finnish Immigrant.* 2000. (Finnish)

Filipovic, Zlata. *Zlata's Diary.* 1994. (Yugoslavian)

Gundisch, Karin. *How I Became an American.* 2001. (Romanian/German)

Joosse, Barbara. *The Morning Chair.* 1995. (Dutch)

Pellowski, Ann. *First Farm in the Valley: Anna's Story.* 1982. (Polish)

Ross, Lillian. *Sarah, also Known as Hannah.* 1994. (Ukrainian)

Sachs, Marilyn. *Call Me Ruth.* 1995. (Russian)

Winter, Jeanette. *Klara's New World.* 1992. (Swedish)

NON-FICTION

Atkin, S. Beth. *Voices from the Fields: Children of Migrant Farmers Tell Their Stories.* 1993.

Bode, Janet. *New Kids on the Block: Oral Histories of Immigrant Teens.* 1989.

Budhos, Marina. *Remix: Conversations with Immigrant Teenagers.* 1999.

Freedman, Russell. *Immigrant Kids.* 1980.

Knippling, Alpana Sharma, ed. *New Immigrant Literatures in the United States.* 1996.

Press, Petra. *A Multicultural Portrait of Immigration.* 1996.

Sandler, Martin W. *Immigrants.* 1995.

Source of Session Plans on Books

Several of the books listed have sessions plans for using them. You can refer to the following websites.

- The Center for Learning at *http://center forlearning.org*
- The International Children's Digital Library at *www.icdlbooks.org*

References

American Immigration Lawyers Association. 2005. "AILA Backgrounder: Myths & Facts in the Immigration Debate." InfoNet:AILA. *www.aila.org*

Bennett, Milton ed. 1998. *Basic Concepts in Intercultural Communication.* Boston: Intercultural Press.

Daynes, Gary. ed. Orchard Simulation adapted from the lesson "The Orchard Experience" from the Edpacket page on the website: *http//:sc.lib.byu.edu/events/fruito flabors/Orchards*

Hill, Margaret. Recording the California Farmworker Story Through Oral History Interviews. SCORE History-Social Science. *http://score.rims.k12.ca.us/score_lessons/ chavez/pages/oral-hist_int_project.html#1*

National Crime Prevention Council. 1994. Quote from "Building and Crossing Bridges: Refugees and Law Enforcement Working Together."

National Gardening Association. 2004. Excerpt from "Service-Learning: Helping Kids and Communities Grow." *Gardens for All,* Vol. 13, No. 1 Spring 2004.

PBS, "In the Mix, the PBS Teen Series"; "Teen Immigrants: 5 American Stories." *www.inthemix.org*

Seelye, H. Ned, ed. 1996. "The Cooperative Map Exercise," pages 133-132, from *Experiential Activities for Intercultural Learning,* Vol. 1. Boston: Intercultural Press.

Youth For Understanding International Exchange. 2005. "Family Values" adapted from *Host Family Handbook.* Washington, DC (pages 11-12)

Youth For Understanding International Exchange. 1994. "Houses of Worship Bulletin Activity" adapted from *Living in the USA Student Workbook.* Washington, DC.